CARP FISHING
ADVANCED TACTICS

CARP FISHING
ADVANCED TACTICS

SIMON CROW

THE CROWOOD PRESS

First published in 2006 by
The Crowood Press Ltd
Ramsbury, Marlborough
Wiltshire SN8 2HR

www.crowood.com

British Library Cataloguing-in-Publication Data
A catalogue record for this book is available from the British Library.

ISBN: 1 86126 877 7
EAN: 978 1 86126 877 8

Dedication
To my old mate Rob Hughes

All photographs by the author, except where indicated otherwise.
Line-drawings by Dave Ramsay of Carp Fishing News Ltd

Edited and designed by
OutHouse!
Shalbourne, Marlborough
Wiltshire SN8 3QJ

Printed by Craft Print International Ltd, Singapore

Contents

Acknowledgements

Where do I start? So many people have helped me over the years. Overall, I perhaps owe the most to Rob Hughes. Ever since we met in a tackle shop in Wolverhampton in 1990 he has been there for me, come rain or shine. Had he not been so busy with his own work, I'm sure he would have been a joint author on this title as he was for the two other books I've produced for Crowood. I don't fish as much with him as I used to but I can safely say that memories of the many great moments we have spent together on the banks will stay with us forever. Let's hope there's a few more in store as we get older. I owe you loads Rob, and I dedicate this book to you.

Similar great mates I owe a lot to are Steve Briggs, Derek Fell and Rene Hawkins. To Steve for putting up with my singing at Lake Raduta and for helping me understand that carp fishing is all about the nice things in life – sleeping, doing a bit more sleeping, maybe making a cup of tea and putting the feet up, and then thinking about re-doing the rods. You're one of the greatest Steve. Thanks to Derek, for whom nothing is ever too much trouble. Like Briggsy, you're one of the most down to earth guys in existence. As for Rene, we've had loads of laughs, especially those about Rob and his golfing exploits. Here's to many more in the future. Ching ching!

In angling, I've had the good fortune to meet many of the big names, but none have had as much influence on me as Rod Hutchinson, Tim Paisley, and Frank Warwick. Rod was a boyhood hero of mine, an angler who inspired me to go out and catch carp. Tim has been a huge inspiration, especially with regards to my career path and showing me that effort equals reward. Frank is an innovator, an incredibly talented and influential angler the world over. He's someone who will make you laugh and keep you entertained, especially with his fluent ramblings in Japanese!

Thanks also to Kev Clifford and Chris Ball of Carp Fishing News Ltd, both of whom inspired me as a young angler with their writings and have since had the faith to employ me. Thanks also to Jon 'Shoes' Jones for his brilliant underwater photographs in Chapter 3, Paddy 'The Jedi Master' Webb at *Carp-Talk*, the Davids at The Bait & Feed Company, Graham Slaughter at Rod Hutchinson Fishing Baits, Pip and Jemima of Angling Publications, Bev at CFN, the many magazine editors who've helped me, Dave Chilton at Kryston, my good friend Christian Finkelde from Germany, my mates outside of angling – Wicko, Claire, Bamber, Hardi, and Glyn, and anyone else I've missed.

Lastly, thanks to my family, whom I love so dearly. To Mom, Bethany, Sharna, Boycie the dog (aka Bosh), Nik, Gaz, Sam, Ted, and Bri. None of you understand a thing about carp fishing, but you've all put up with my ramblings and helped me along the way.

Introduction

I can hardly believe it's almost ten years since Rob Hughes and I wrote *Strategic Carp Fishing*, our first book for The Crowood Press. That book was aimed at the intermediate carper; our second title, *Discover Carp Fishing*, published some five years later, targeted the beginner. This book is slightly more advanced than *Strategic Carp Fishing*, the next step up if you like, but one that both the novice and intermediate carper will be able to relate to.

Much of what we wrote in *Strategic Carp Fishing* is still relevant, but with the passage of time comes change. Carp fishing is now a huge business, worth hundreds of millions of pounds per year the world over. So much time has been spent on developing new rods, baits, lines and equipment that the approach of the angler in the 21st century is so, so different to what it was in the 20th. If you have read *Discover Carp Fishing*, and have a very good knowledge of the basics, then get your teeth into what is contained herein. I have tried to make this book as bang up-to-date as I can, full of fresh information that I know will help you catch carp from the easiest of the easy lakes all the way through to the hardest of the hard.

Unfortunately Rob hasn't joined me as co-author, although you will see him appearing here and there in some of the chapters. Everything is therefore based on my own carp fishing experience, something that is advancing each and every time I step on to the banks. Apart from three interviews conducted with other anglers, everything is in my own words. It is my outlook on the sport and how I go about catching fish, all based on the belief that the carp is a very simple creature and that each and every water and situation is different. If you follow that line of thought throughout your angling, I guarantee you won't be far off the mark.

Enjoy your season, wherever you fish, and catch a few along the way.

Author Simon Crow with a Linear Fisheries mid-thirty mirror from Hardwick Lake.

1 The Way of the Carp

WHAT IS ANGLING PRESSURE?

This is an incredibly difficult question to answer since angling pressure can be defined as both direct and indirect. Let me explain. A carp that has never been caught can still be subject to angling pressure since it can sense danger as noises on the bank, obstacles in the water, or even signals that are passed to it via other fish. Carp are masters of their own environments, having a knowledge of every single nook and cranny within their home. They may visit certain areas of a lake or water only occasionally, but you can bet your last dollar they will know when something isn't quite right about it.

At the extreme end of the angling pressure scale there are big-fish waters that have anglers around each and every day of the year – if not fishing, just looking for the fish. On most of these venues, such as the Yateley Car Park Lake, which is about 20 acres (9ha) in size with about 20 big fish within, the carp live a very nice life feeding regularly on anglers' baits – growing

A group of very pressured carp huddle safely in a snag, well away from anglers.

steadily and healthily. Such waters are fished most of the year by very dedicated anglers who watch the fish and learn from them every day. They know their movements. They know where they feed. They know the places they frequent the most. Basically, they know everything about them, and the carp have learned to adapt themselves as a result.

It is a well-known fact that fish subject to the amount of pressure that the Car Park Lake sees have a habit of avoiding capture. They have become so accustomed to the rigs and bait the anglers use that their ability to associate them with danger has become highly developed, enabling them to detect which items to avoid and which ones to pick up. In many cases, carp in these waters are renowned for picking up every single free offering of bait made available to them, totally avoiding the hookbait amongst them. Anglers call this phenomenon being 'cleaned out', a phrase that refers to carp that have cleaned up all of the free offerings without so much as a lift on the indicator.

The folklore amongst anglers seems to be that carp that have cleaned out will have sampled the hookbait – i.e., pulled the rig back and sensed some kind of tension on the bait. Having watched countless carp feeding on bait, however, it is my opinion that it doesn't always happen like that. Yes, there are many occasions when the carp will come into a baited area, sample the hookbait and eject it, but I tend to think that most of the time they just leave it well alone, using a sixth sense to tell them that something isn't quite right about that particular item.

It isn't just at hard-fished waters that I have experienced being cleaned out either.

When you've anglers braving the elements like this, you can guess the carp in this venue are very pressured.

Even at less-pressured waters I have seen it happen. Some of the hardest fish I have ever come face to face with were the type that live in the old estate lake waters that lie in the middle of nowhere and are rarely fished: the sort of venue where the only man-made sound you hear is of a distant aeroplane or tractor. I know it may sound strange, but I actually think that the carp in these waters know when something is not quite right about their environment as soon as an angler sets foot on the bank. I've witnessed carp spook off as I have crept silently along the bank well back from the water's edge, and I am left standing in amazement, wondering what on earth it was I did to make them aware of my presence.

The nature of a venue has so much to do with the way in which the carp react to

An Orchid Lake mirror known as BJ, which weighed 29lb 12oz on this occasion. A week later the same fish was caught again at 30lb 14oz.

angler presence that a precise definition of angling pressure is almost impossible in the limited space available in this book. The carp in some waters don't have many anglers targeting them, so the pressure the fish respond to will be completely different to that where anglers are present every single day of the year. At waters where the stocking density is quite high, and competition for food resources correspondingly high, they will also be more willing to play the percentage game, taking the chances they wouldn't otherwise do where safe food is readily available to them. We've then also to consider that in addition to the influence venues have on pressure, every single carp is different. Each one goes about its daily routine, and reacts to what the anglers do, in its own individual way. Carp have their own personalities, but this topic in its own right deserves some serious discussion because it is quite easy to label individual fish with identities that really aren't representative of their true character.

HOW INTELLIGENT ARE CARP?

Let me put this question a different way. Is a carp that frequently visits the bank smart because it knows it is going to get put back once it has had a nice feed on anglers' baits? Or is it a 'mug' because it gets caught so much?

To me, a carp is a very simple creature, albeit I think there are different personalities (so-to-say) from fish to fish. I know that might sound like a weird thing to say, but, in all honesty, how can two carp be the same? No two dogs are the same, and that also goes for other pets or wild creatures such as cats, cows, foxes, or whatever. You've only to look at tank fish to see what I'm getting at, or sit in a tree and watch a

group of fish feeding. There will be different personalities amongst them. Some will be aggressive, some will be shy. Some will be away from the group, whilst some will stick with others at all times. If we take a look at our own lakes and venues that we fish on a regular basis, with time we will all be able to identify the 'mug' fish as well as the 'once-a-year' fish, or even, in some cases, the 'never-get-caught' fish. Why would they appear so different if they didn't have their own personalities?

I used to think that carp were all the same. They all liked the same foods, they all tended to get caught at one time or another, and so on. Now, after many years of carp fishing and reading up on the species, I think differently. For instance, I know there are carp that just do not eat anglers' bait. Some people say that these fish are the cutest of them all, which may well be right, but, for me, this is crediting the carp with more intelligence than I

A big mirror makes its way slowly to the net, its first capture of the season, but why did it make the mistake?

11

Don't fall short in the bait department. Big old fish that have been around for years will know the difference between quality and low-nutrient bait.

think it (as a species) possesses. I think it is not that these fish are necessarily cute, but rather that they are not turned on by the baits being used at a water. They perhaps don't have a liking for the ingredients, the smell or whatever. Having been brought up on only one or a handful of natural foods, they may not have the inquisitive nature to change to, or even sample, something different.

I think that some fish are caught more than others because they have a liking for a certain bait; it is not just that they are 'mug' fish. Perhaps a certain ingredient is more stimulating to them. I know for certain that I could go to some of my old haunts and catch some of my old favourite fish again and again, simply by selecting a bait that I know they are susceptible to.

A Birch Grove 30lb 12oz mirror taken during a freezing-cold late-November morning. This fish hadn't been caught during the winter for a long while.

That's not to say they can only be caught on one bait, but that they, like other wild animals, are stimulated by certain food stuffs more than others. Most lakes go through bait cycles each year, generally according to the latest trends. One year, the going bait is this, and the next it is that. It may be these cycles have an effect on which fish get caught each year. If I think about myself, which I know I shouldn't when considering carp, I know that when I smell Indian food, my stomach turns over. I absolutely hate it. Let me smell Chinese food, cakes or biscuits though, and my mouth is watering like a dripping tap. I honestly think the same happens with carp and that the baits being used have a huge bearing on which fish visit the bank the most that season.

Perhaps another explanation for why some fish are caught more often is that they recognize certain baits as being more nutritious for them. I know a lot of people have knocked the subject of HNV (High Nutritive Value) baits in the past, but many of the knockers (I was one once) have since realized the importance of using a quality bait when angling for pressured fish. I don't know why carp prefer baits that have more of a balanced nature to them, but they absolutely do. As an example, these days you will not consistently catch big UK carp from tough venues on cheap 50/50 soya/semolina baits with high attraction levels. You will be able to catch smaller carp for sure, but for plenty of years now the evidence proves that the bigger fish consistently fall for the nutritious

It is absolutely baffling why some carp go uncaught for years. Are they just cute? Or is it just that anglers are not trying hard enough?

ones. Why this is so, I don't exactly know, but I relate it to the fact that the older the fish get the more they recognize what is good for them. Basically, they are wiser. Young kids generally like only rubbish foods and won't try things that are good for them until they grow older. We might be like this because we are domesticated,

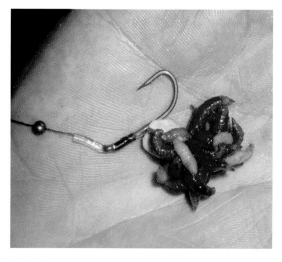

Will the best rigs in the game outsmart even the smartest of carp when their guard is up?

Even the best indicators will only help you so far if the fish are not playing ball.

but science has proved that wild animals have recognition instincts that are much more well defined than those of humans.

If I think back to my winter fishing, which is where bait recognition instinct has been more noticeable to me, on the waters where I've fished consecutive years I can recall that certain fish were definitely more susceptible to particular baits. A lot of waters tend to see the same baits and tactics in the winter – the glugged single hook-baits, the low fishmeal baits, and so on – resulting in the same old faces getting caught. I remember when I first joined the winter syndicate at Birch Grove, I ended up catching one or two fish that prompted the occasional comment, 'Oh, I haven't seen that one in the winter before.' Back then, most of the lads who fished there were using the in-vogue winter baits and strategies. I went in with something different – methods and baits that the water hadn't seen for a while – and I am convinced this was a major factor in why I caught very few fish, but bigger and older ones.

Despite these beliefs, however, if we go deeper into this intriguing topic I actually believe that a fish's susceptibility to capture is also determined by its inner traits. For instance, not all big fish get caught year after year. Some go uncaught for years, sometimes starting the rumours of one being dead or having been stolen. I remember a few years ago when Yorkshire's Motorway Pond 'Biggun' hadn't been caught for some time. I heard all sorts of rumours about its being dead, tethered in snags, and so on. Low and behold, the fish was caught some time later at a new all-time high of over 40lb, well up on its previous best weight. I don't think Biggun is necessarily any cuter than any other carp in Motorway. If it was, it wouldn't get caught at all. I believe that compared to some of the other fish in the lake it is just a little bit less aggressive about feeding.

Obviously there are big fish that are quite the opposite of Biggun. Mary, the former British record mirror, was very susceptible to capture during its famous years at the top of the carp world. Wraysbury, where it swam, is one of the richest carp waters around, but Mary still liked to feed on anglers' baits on a regular basis. Some would say it thrived on them, but I don't think that was quite the case. The great fish grew almost 20lb in a period of four or five years between captures in its early years in Wraysbury, a time when, I believe, very little bait was being introduced. For me, Mary was just a greedy fish and very confident with it as well. I know from having fished the venue when the fish was alive, it certainly liked to travel around the lake a

Frank Warwick with a 30lb-plus winter mirror, which gave just a slight lift on the indicator.

fair bit. One minute it would be in the North Lake and the next it would be in the South, right down in Bryants Bay. Perhaps the mere fact that it did so much travelling meant that it had to feed more regularly. I don't know, I'm just speculating. One thing I do know is that it certainly had a lot of confidence because, when you saw it, it

Make the fish want your bait so much that they make the mistake.

never appeared to bolt off like a lot of others in the lake. Instead, it would just glide away until you were out of sight.

Although I'm a big believer in this personality thing with carp, I also think that carp are very simple creatures: they will always be attracted to items they recognize as food. This is why bait is, after location, the most important aspect of the angler's armoury. If a carp isn't attracted to something, it isn't going to pick it up. Many people will disagree with me there but, to me, a rig only has to be capable of hooking and landing a fish. So long as the rig and hookbait are as discreet as possible, and as anti-eject as I think I can get them, I'm confident. A good bait and a well-thought-out strategy of how to apply it can get a carp to drop its guard more than any commercial rig item. Certainly carp can be rig shy. I've witnessed them being very finicky at plenty of different waters. A slight lift on the indicator, or a twitch of the tip, has been carp on so many occasions that I've lost count. I'm not convinced, though, that when carp are feeding with their guard up, we can do things with rigs to turn these twitches or whatever into full-blooded takes. We can fiddle around with hair lengths and hooklinks, as well as hook patterns, and so on, occasionally benefiting from the changes, but that's not the point I'm trying to make. I'm talking about the times when we have drained our resources, and are using a rig that we know is 100 per cent right. When the carp are not 'playing ball' at these times, there is just nothing we can do with a rig to make things better. Sometimes, we may catch one off guard by being quick on the rods, but for me that is all we can do – other than sit on our hands and wait for the storm to pass.

The best thing to do is to try to prevent the finicky periods arising in the first place. A well thought-out baiting campaign is one of the best ways of doing this. Make the fish

16

want your bait so much that they drop their guard. Build up their confidence on it, and in the areas that you are applying it. Even this, though, isn't always enough, since I really do believe that carp have, especially when they have been under severe pressure, a sixth sense that tells them when something just isn't quite right about an area. These are the times when you will find them cleaning you out, and you haven't even a hint of what is going on until it's happened. Perhaps a line in the water is vibrating, or possibly a hookbait stands out like a sore thumb. Whatever the reason, the fish just know that something isn't right, and this prompts them to be on their best behaviour and careful in what they pick up or consider picking up. These are the periods of very difficult fishing.

At the opposite end of the scale, and to really contradict everything I have said above, there will be times when the carp act quite out of character and you can't understand why they are doing so. This is one of the amazing things about carp fishing. As suddenly as a light switch being flicked, the fish that normally laugh at the rigs and baits being thrown at them suddenly start getting caught, almost throwing themselves at the anglers, making their captures look so easy it will amaze you that they are so difficult at other times. This may be for any one of a million reasons, such as a decrease in natural foods meaning they have to turn to anglers' baits, or a stimulation caused by the weather. There is also the chance that the fish may be unwell, when perhaps old age or illness has taken over. Such windows of opportunity are usually small. More prolonged changes in character are usually the sign of worse things to come. I spoke to big-fish angler Steve Allcott shortly after the former British record mirror Mary died. He told me he thought something was up with him/her before the great fish passed away.

A wily Birch Grove mid-thirty. This tough fish from a very tough water came ten minutes after casting out!

He'd seen it in several different snags around the lake, which really wasn't the norm. Another example I can think of is Orchid Lake's Leather, which generally only ever got caught a couple of times a year maximum. As if something untoward had happened to it, in its last year of life it visited the bank no fewer than a dozen times in the space of twelve months.

THE UNCAUGHT CARP

In England we know which fish are caught more regularly than others from our waters because so many anglers fish and keep records of what is happening. We also have venues where it is possible to see and keep track of individual fish. If the waters in England were any bigger and the anglers couldn't, with their own eyes, see the fish actually swimming, I have no doubt that the topic of uncaught carp would barely be taken seriously.

For years, anglers have talked about venues that contain carp that just don't feed on anglers' baits, even at waters where the stocking density is at such a level that the fish really need to compete to maintain a healthy lifestyle. Perhaps the most famous sighting of an uncaught biggie was back in the days of The Carp Catchers Club when Dick Walker wrote about the possibility of there being an uncaught monster in the legendary Redmire Pool. A photograph was even taken by one of the members of the early syndicate of a fish that was said to be a giant leviathan con-

sistently avoiding capture. In more recent times, several notable anglers have seen similar uncaught fish at venues such as Wraysbury, where there was talk of a leathery fish known as Waddle, which appeared to be bigger than Mary.

Uncaught carp exist not just because anglers like to dream about there being such fish in a water, but because there are many, many examples of their existing and out-smarting even the best anglers in the land. Take the legendary Longfield Pool as an example, a water that was very, very pressured in the late 1970s and early to mid-1980s. It was fished by some of the country's leading anglers of the time, all highly acclaimed, thinking anglers who knew how to outwit some of the most wily

Wraysbury, one of the toughest lakes in the land, and home to uncaught carp for certain.

Uncaught carp undoubtedly exist: anglers have seen them with their own eyes.

carp. It was only a small water of about 20 acres (9ha) in size, but it was very rich and extremely difficult. Every day of the year it had about twenty dedicated anglers around it. Anyone who caught a fish out of there was very fortunate, and the regular anglers believed they knew every carp that was in there. That was, until they drained it down to remove all of the fish when the fishery was to close. Amazingly, they discovered at least half a dozen fish to almost 30lb which had never graced the banks!

The carp is an amazing freshwater fish, and no other species in the angling world is quite so addictive. Everything I discuss in this book is based on the belief that the carp is a wild animal with wild instincts. Each is different and each one has a personality, which is influenced by the nature of the environment it resides in as well as by its innate characteristics. Treat them as stupid creatures and they will take the Mickey out of you. Treat them with too much caution and they will happily do the same.

2 The Carp Angler's Calendar

There is no denying that as the seasons progress, the angler needs to adapt his tactics to suit the conditions relevant to the time of the year. In this chapter I wish to take a month by month look at the carping calendar and try to give you an insight into some of the thinking that goes into being a successful all-round carp angler. Although there are no hard and fast rules for each month, there are general pointers that will help you during the season.

JANUARY AND FEBRUARY

For me, January has always been a month that is quite unpredictable. The build-up to Christmas always sees a number of excel-

January, an unpredictable month weather-wise. Your water-craft skills will be tested to the limit.

lent fish caught, and a quick flick through an early January issue of *Carp-Talk* will reveal this. The issues that go out at the beginning and in the middle of the month will have been put to bed at the end of December – on the back of one of the best winter feeding periods in the carp angler's calendar. Compare these news pages with those of issues that come out towards the back end of January, when only the die-hards and overseas carpers remain.

You can never be sure what the weather is going to do in January, which I think is the main reason for the lapse in catch reports, even from the super-keenies. During my career, I have spent quite a few New Year's Eves on the bank, experiencing both really cold and mild spells, but, to be fair, the earlier part of the month has usually been kinder to me than the end. At Birch Grove in Shropshire at the turn of the century I actually began the year very well with a low-thirty on New Year's Day morning. It was one of those sessions when I had to put the effort in, arriving at the lake for 5 a.m. after a drive from Yorkshire on roads that were completely devoid of traffic. I was set up in twenty minutes or so, with the rod going off shortly before first light, resulting in my having perhaps the meaningless claim of being the first angler in the UK to have caught a thirty-pounder that year.

I also have several other fond memories of catching good fish in January, again including weights over 30lb. But these results have probably had little to do with when I have been out on the bank, or the weather conditions I have endured whilst there; the one main thing they have in common is that all came from winter holding areas.

Winter Holding Areas

You tend to find that carp love the same places in the winter, year after year, unless a venue takes on board changes to its environment. As an example, at Orchid Lakes in Oxfordshire, a venue I know quite well, for many years the fish used to love holding up in a large reed bed that encroached into the lake. When Marsh Pratley took over the water, however, he set about trying to improve the fishery as a winter venue, so the first thing he did was to cut back the reed bed so there was nothing for the fish to hold up in. A couple of seasons on from when Marsh took over, the lake's reputation as a tough winter venue had changed to that of one of the most productive in the country. I think in the winter of 2002/3 alone Orchid produced something like 200 twenties in December,

A 30lb 8oz mirror from Birch Grove on 1 January, a nice way to start the year.

January and February, a figure that is remarkable for any fishery in the UK. Of these fish, at least twenty of them were thirty-pounders, so my first piece of advice to anyone wanting to catch themselves a good fish in January is make sure you choose the right venue. Place the odds in your favour and go after fish that are catchable in the month you are fishing.

I have always found that carp really love to feel safe in the winter months. If you have any sunken features to fish to then these would have to be the first place I would turn my attention. Big carp, especially, bully the other fish, so they usually get the first pick of any holding areas that may be available. I remember fishing on Withy Pool in Bedfordshire where it was clear that the bigger fish were the bosses. They could always be seen right at the back of the snags in the cubbyholes that were hidden away, and you would never see any of the other fish in these spots; it was as though they had marked their territory and the others identified that.

Examples are always going to be site-specific, but it's likely that if there are one or two big fish in a water then these may behave like the fish in Withy. There may be one or two areas they will frequent, so try to track these down. Look under every bush and in every corner of the lake every time you visit, trying to uncover the patterns and behaviour of the fish. Even in the winter time, there will be signs that will help you, even if it's just information gleaned from other anglers and not your own first-hand experiences. Any bit of info will help you no end, even the misleading stuff.

It is an instinct of a wild fish to overwinter in an area where it feels comfortable and less vulnerable to predation. Not every water has areas of cover, but even in a goldfish-bowl-type fishery, the carp will warm to one particular area – even if it's just mid-water off the bottom.

A 28lb 12oz Orchid Lake mirror, one of the many specimen fish caught from the lake during January after the owner thinned out a thick reed bed.

Here's a look at some of my favourite areas to target in January, in order of preference:

Snags
Close to sunken trees or broken branches have to be the first places I would choose to look. So attractive are they that I've even seen big carp congregate around the snags in 2ft (60cm) of water in the winter, preferring them to the deeper sections of lake (which went down to 7ft/2m in places).

Weed Beds
Lakes that are especially weedy in the summer are likely to contain strands and

blooms of weed even in the colder months. Tough weeds such as Canadian Pondweed and Milfoil will quite happily overwinter in the UK, offering great areas for the larger carp to hide away. *Carp-Talk* often receives reports of big fish, especially thirties, being caught from clear areas surrounded by weed beds.

Silty Areas
It is well known that although deep silty areas of lakes are not a snaggy feature, some great catches are made from them. Top day-ticket waters – Farlows Lake in Buckinghamshire and St Johns Pool in Oxfordshire are two examples – produce good thirties in the winter months to baits fished over deep silty areas of bottom. The silt areas in front of Heron's Point have traditionally fished well at Farlows, as indeed has the silt bed out in front of the road bank at St Johns.

Reed Beds
Carp love to get amongst thick sets of reeds in cold water as they offer them shelter from all directions. The larger a set of reeds the better, especially those that branch out over varying depths of water. Some reed types actually float on the surface in huge rafts, creating a great shelter for the carp. Orchid Lakes, even today, still produces good thirties in January from baits tight to the reeds, often from single hookbaits alongside small stringers.

Islands
Areas that are out of bounds to humans are always a great place to fish, even if there are no visible sunken branches, reed

Right in amongst the snags, where they feel safest.

beds or weed close by. Most islands have shelves around the side, offering the carp a variety of depth, which will be a big attraction if there is nothing else to pull them in. A great place to try is the side of the island that catches the most rays from the sun – such an area once produced for me a nice winter 30lb common from a bait fished in 2ft (60cm) of water.

Dying Lily Beds

If there are lilies at your lake, then the chances are that when they die back there will still be a few shoots sprouting up off the bottom. The rhizomes of lilies never die completely, and the shoots and leaves that remain not only offer shelter to big carp but attract a few food items, such as snails and crustaceans, which the carp will feed upon. The pads at Birch Grove have often produced big winter fish in the past, including thirties.

The Big Freeze

I always find February to be a very difficult month to catch carp of any size, let alone the bigger fish. It is a month when heavy frosts can arrive at any time, and also a period of the carp angler's calendar when fishing can be lost to lakes being frozen in. When I was a member of the Birch Grove winter syndicate, which generally ran from 1 November until 31 March, I can remember Tim Paisley extending the fishing on the famous lake to compensate members for the loss of most of February. The lake was enclosed in trees and, as soon as the

The sun is high in the sky and the fish are in the margins, taking it all in.

temperature plummeted, it was quite normal for it to be locked underneath a thick sheet of ice.

Living in Yorkshire I was over two hours' drive away from Birch, which meant that on some occasions I drove down to the lake not really knowing what state it would be in. Some would say that I wasted a lot of time as I often found it under ice, but even walking round a lake in that condition gave away one or two secrets which in the long-run really helped me to piece together the jigsaw that catching big fish consistently can be.

Having seen Rob Hughes bank an amazing 30lb-plus common from under the ice previously, I'd actually remained on the lake on several occasions when it froze over my baits. During the initial stages of freezing at Birch I'd noted that for the first day or so, the whole lake would freeze over, yet a day or so later, depending on how severe the weather was, two or three spots out in the middle were being melted by the water underneath. I think it was the third time I'd arrived to find it frozen but with the two or three areas ice-free again that I managed to put the pieces of this particular jigsaw together. These spots weren't in the margins and definitely hadn't been made by the activity of the birds, but instead were right in the middle of the lake over deep water of 15ft (4.5m).

When a lake freezes over, the water underneath will be a maximum of 4°C (39°F) if it remains with a lid. For Birch to be melting in isolated areas, the water underneath these spots had to be slightly warmer than this, and it had to be trickling in because it wasn't uncommon for the lake to freeze over completely, only for the spots to slowly start to melt through a day or so later. Birch has a massive history, not only as a carp water but as a lake for its own sake. After chatting with several people in the region, I discovered it dated back to the ice age and was spring fed. Spring water remains at a fairly constant temperature throughout the year, generally around 5–6°C (41–43°F) in the winter. It didn't take a scientist to work out that the melted spots were being caused by the springs coming up through the lake bed. Pin-pointing the location of these therefore could be very, very useful for my winter carp fishing, as these areas were potentially the warmer spots around which the fish may huddle.

To cut a long story short, one of these particular springs proved a very productive spot for me, producing a string of very big fish, including five winter thirties, from ten takes. It was a big fish spot that had a habit of doing the thirty-pounders. Quite why the bigger fish liked it there I couldn't exactly say, but I know from speaking to lots of different anglers and also having fished lots of different lakes, whatever the time of the year, big fish of 30lb-plus more often than not get caught from the same areas of a lake. Obviously finding these spots isn't always easy, but if ever you find yourself in the situation of being frozen in, yet you really get the bug to be out on the banks, follow your instincts at least for a walk round because you never know what you may come across.

Mid-Water Carp – Pull Them Down!

To pull the mid-water resting Birch Grove carp down, Rob Hughes and I devised a method of attraction that I shall run through now. First soak some rig foam in boiling hot flavour/attractor. Soak it for two to three minutes, then insert it into a swim feeder (use some forceps to do this). Then attach the feeder to your rig. Now place the feeder into a PVA bag, tie the top, and cast the whole lot out, combined with your normal rig. The PVA bag basically acts as protection for a couple of minutes until the

Frozen in, but there are still signs that are worthy of note.

There's movement under that ice!

rig is on the bottom, but, once it has dissolved, the warm attractor in the feeder will rise from the bottom up the water column, dispersing attraction at all levels. It won't stay warm for very long because of the temperature of the surrounding lake water, but it will have dispersed enough attraction to tell the carp that something smells nice on the bottom, hopefully pulling them down for an inspection. This method is ideal on a roving rod, which gets redone every hour or so.

February success in the shape of a Lincolnshire low-thirty common taken from shallow water.

A great way to pull mid-water carp down for an investigation.

MARCH AND APRIL

Pre-Baiting for Long-Term Benefits

March is the time of year when the carp in the UK begin to wake up after their dormant winter spell. It is a time when you really have to set the foundations for a campaign if you want to catch fish consistently throughout the year. A brilliant tactic for anglers who concentrate their efforts on one particular water is to formulate a pre-baiting campaign, starting it any time now.

It takes a lot of effort to visit a lake on a regular basis in between fishing sessions to

Carp in the shallows – a good indicator that winter is almost over.

pre-bait, and it also costs a fair amount of money to keep it going in. Perhaps this is the main reason why so few people seem to do it. If I think back to all of the waters I have baited on a regular basis, no one other than me has gone to the trouble of doing it. Starting any baiting campaign usually begins with doubts about whether the effort is justified – is it worth it? After all, most of us would rather go to the lake to fish than merely to introduce some bait. It can be very easy to look at the short-term inconvenience rather than the longer-term benefits of pre-baiting. The early days, in fact, can see you completely demoralized if nothing comes as quickly as you want it to,

Essential baiting-up gear: spod rod, marker float and the bait itself.

so it is very much a tactic suited to the strong minded. Once, I baited a water from the middle of March all the way through to the opening week in mid-June, watching the fish absolutely gorge the bait during the closed season only to see them switch off it come opening day. I was left scratching my head a week into the season, and I lost all faith because other anglers around me were catching. I've since learnt that the benefits of any pre-baiting campaign are usually not realized until a week or so into the season. Basically, the number of other baits being introduced by anglers at the start of the season usually sees the fish tempted to alter their feeding preferences until they begin to identify the pre-baited food as safer.

The Pre-Bait

So what sort of baits are suited to pre-baiting? If you ask me, any free bait that the carp can get hold of will obviously boost their confidence, even on very pressured waters where a lot of bait gets introduced on a regular basis. 'Any bait', however, usually lifts the confidence of the fish in the areas it is applied rather than making them want a specific bait. For this reason, I will say that I much prefer to choose what is generally regarded as 'food baits' – quality food items that will make the carp feel good about eating them. To give you an idea, at Motorway Pond, my early season water for this year (2006), I have been applying a well-balanced mix that is high-energy and nutritious, and already I am seeing some results for my efforts. I started baiting the lake in the middle of March when I was there for a three-day blank, steadily increasing the amount on a weekly basis. I've been baiting the venue with the MC Addicted Mix from the Bait & Feed Company – the same bait I caught with at the water two seasons earlier when I didn't pre-bait. I consider baits to have a three-year life span on a water, the third year being when results start to taper off. I'm not looking to get three years out of this bait, just a few more months while I pay the venue some attention or until I get the fish I am after on the bank. From the few trips I had made to the venue previously, I know it works well and therefore see no need to change it just yet.

I've been backing up the boilies with hemp – the pre-cooked sort by Dynamite – a bait that is instantly attractive and that works very well as a pre-bait alongside boilies. Some people may question using a particle as a pre-bait because you could be baiting for other anglers, but in my experience there is definitely something about using hemp alongside a good-quality food bait in such an instance. Perhaps it's the mix of natural and artificial attractors, I don't know, but it is one combination that I hear a lot of positive results about. One item I don't like pre-baiting with is pellet. I find this a great bait to fish over when short-session fishing or when area-baiting a large water but, long term, I think it can be wasted since the smaller nuisance fish get accustomed to where it is being introduced, in much the same way as carp do boilies. There are obviously benefits to attracting such fish into the swim but, for me, if I'm going to go to the lengths of pre-baiting I want to know that when I get to fish I will more than likely catch my target species.

Where to Pre-Bait
At some venues I think that pre-baiting anywhere in a lake can be of benefit to the fishing because the primary aim of doing it is to get the carp used to seeing your feed. This is part of building up their confidence. However, at a low-stock water, I don't believe that this approach is the right way to go. At this type of water the fish will be very particular about where they visit on a daily basis, and I've come to

know that bait in certain areas of these lakes is just wasted. It has to be in the line of their patrol routes as well as where they feed on natural food. Plumbing and dragging a lead can work wonders for you here, as can getting out in the boat and checking the depths, looking for signs. The early part of March is likely to have very good water clarity because the fish activity may still be quite patchy. Be on the lookout for undulations in the lake bed, preferably round-like craters 12in (30cm) or more deeper than the surrounding bottom. All lakes will have them, I guarantee it, features that will have been created by the foraging of the carp. The food items

Pellets: not one of my favourites for pre-baiting.

Late March 29lb common from a marginal patrol route.

are sometimes locked up in the lake bed as much as a couple of feet down because larvae such as the bloodworm feel safest depositing their eggs there.

When it comes to actually fishing over the pre-bait, I don't fish over a large area: I prefer to target one fish at a time with a handful or two around a hookbait just for recognition. A large baited area will usually attract several carp into the swim, and a hooked one from amongst them will soon spread the danger message. Even down to the very finer points, such as hookbait choice, I try to increase the odds in my favour. I therefore don't use hookbaits that are different from the food I have been feeding them. Pop-ups are something I will turn a blind eye to, preferring to go in with a standard bottom bait, which is balanced to act exactly like a free offering.

Opportunist Moments

The aim with pre-baiting is to raise the fishes' confidence in the food you are introducing, so it stands to reason that you should allow the fish enough time to get accustomed to it. I wouldn't fish over any pre-bait until April, allowing at least two to three weeks of introduction to have passed. Besides, March is a transition month really because you can be sure that at some stage during its thirty-one days the fish will begin to move out of their winter holding

A depression in the lake bed surrounded by weed, almost certainly a feature created by the carp.

areas and into the other parts of the lake where you will be able to tempt them with roving rods quite successfully.

I'm of the opinion that the bigger fish tend to wake up slightly later than the smaller residents. It may only be a few days or so, but the bigger fish in almost all waters get caught out a little later than when a venue is deemed to have 'switched on'. It happens all over the country, and a great way of checking the form is to take a look at *Carp-Talk* each week. As the year moves into March, you will see the number of catch reports increase from February, with an obvious boost in thirties as the month progresses.

Keep an eye out for fish crashing and rolling, trying to rid themselves of parasites such as leaches, which will have attached themselves to their flanks during the cold weather when they were resting up. The bigger 30lb-plus fish won't crash clear out of the water as much as the younger smaller fish, but you can be sure they will be

This 28lb mirror gave its location away by popping its head out shortly before picking up a PVA bag cast close by.

Late April at Orchid Lake and the carp are showing all over the place.

A bit of everything in a bag helps to confuse them.

You still see very few anglers using big hookbaits.

amongst them, so keep your eyes peeled and your ears open. The biggies are likely to waddle across the water's surface or just poke their heads out enough to show they are still there. When you see one do this, react immediately and get a bait on it!

The carp will be waking up from a dormant winter, so they will be very inquisitive about anything that smells like food. A wily thirty, however, will still have its guard raised if it has graced the bank many times in the past. It therefore pays to do something slightly different to what the other anglers around you are favouring with their presentation, especially if you are using a roaming rod to cast at showing fish. Here are a few pointers:

• I rate PVA traps for my roving rods in March. The 30lb carp are likely to have fairly big mouths compared to smaller fish, so a bag the size of a ping-pong ball would be my preference if I was targeting one of the bigger fish.
• This bag presentation is aiming to offer a thirty a mouthful of food. I favour crushed boilies and pellets for this, rather than just pellets.
• I would opt for some crushed baits of different colours, sizes and smells. There will be some yellows, reds and browns in there, some that are fishy, others livery and some fruity. In short, I favour anything that offers a complex food smell as this may not be so attractive to the smaller carp but may be inviting to a biggie, which has well-tested taste buds.
• On the hook, I would go for a big bait, something like a 20–24mm size. So few anglers use bait of this size these days that I'm convinced some just don't believe they are acceptable. Take it from me: a big carp will take a big hookbait with pleasure, much as they would a large crayfish or swan mussel.

- For this presentation, you will need a short hooklink of 6in, preferably one that is supple and fits in well with the mouthful of bait theory. I rate Kryston's Super Nova 25lb for this.
- When using a big bait on the hook, to stand a chance of pricking the fish you will need a size 6 hook minimum combined with a self-hooking rig. I

actually prefer a size 4 to a 6, but I certainly wouldn't go in with one smaller than that.

Déjà Vu

You generally find that once April arrives, the fish visit the same areas of the lake that they did at the same time the previous year.

I caught this low-twenty the previous year – almost exactly to the day – and from the same spot.

Bottoms up – the annual cycle of the lake bed turning over – is a great indicator that the spring has arrived.

Two seasons ago I fished the start of April on Dolly Mill, one of Rod Hutchinson's syndicate waters. I fished two sessions there in April, an over-nighter at the beginning, which proved a blank, and a three-dayer towards the end of the week, which produced three fish. On both occasions, I fished various areas of the lake as I tried to search out where the carp may be and where they would pick up baits. The weather at the beginning of the week was fairly cold and chilly with no fish activity, but, during the latter half, as soon as the sun got higher and warmer in the sky, the dark submarines from the depths below soon started to make themselves visible.

My second visit proved to be an almost mirror picture of a session I had had there at around the same time the previous year.

In the same weather conditions, I managed three fish from exactly the same spots that I caught from the previous year, with all pick-ups coming at almost exactly the same time of the day – I had all three fish from an area of shallow water at the bottom end of the lake and within inches of one another. They also fell to the same tactics – single MC Addicted pop-ups over the top of a handful of the Bait & Feed Company's High Betaine pellets – and, strangely enough, they all came shortly after the 'bottoms up' effect had started its annual cycle, which had also been apparent the previous year. Coincidence or just the predictability of carp fishing?

On top of this I had another weird, déjà vu experience during that session at Dolly. There I was minding my own business

Big-fish angler Alijn Danau uses the buds on the trees to tell him when the fish will be munching.

looking out across the water, having not seen any signs of fish. Then, low and behold, I saw one that turned out to be the same one I saw first the previous April – the venue's big linear. It drifted into exactly the same spot, up-ended in exactly the same place, had a bit of a rummage, and then waddled off, not to be seen again that day. It was an amazing experience and, like before, a frustrating one because I wasn't prepared for it and therefore couldn't exploit the situation.

It's not just at the Mill that I have had incidents like this happen. The longer you fish on a water, the more the annual similarities of each session become apparent and the more you realize how important it is to understand the lifestyle of the carp in the water you are targeting. More often than not the weather plays the greatest part in the annual cycle of sport on any lake and, so long as you keep your eyes open, it may even be possible to stay one step ahead

of the pack with regards to knowing where to place your hookbaits at a certain time. To give you an example, bottoms up is a good indicator that the carp are moving into the shallower water. The first signs of this taking place usually sees me positioning my hookbait away from the overwintering spots and more towards the early spring ones. Shallow parts of the lake are a favourite area I like to fish as soon as I see signs of bottoms up, because you can almost guarantee that it means the water has warmed up and, even in between bursts of cold weather, will not drop any lower for a considerable number of weeks.

I have had some great early spring catches using bottoms up as an indicator, and I know several other anglers rate it as a good sign that the seasons have changed. I can remember former British record holder Lee Jackson at one of the NEC Go Fishing shows giving a detailed account of looking for signs of bottoms up as well as reading other signs from nature. A couple of years ago I also spent some time on the bank with Belgian big-fish ace Alijn Danau while doing an interview for a feature. I recall Alijn saying that he doesn't fish at all during the winter, only starting when the buds on the trees have started to open up and the turnover of the lake bed has began.

MAY AND JUNE

Full Steam Ahead!

The big fish months of May and June have to be the period of the year when I'd say 75 per cent of UK anglers catch their person-

Derek Fell with an early-May capture of East Yorkshire's Tilery Lake big mirror known as the Black Fish.

al best carp. English carp angling legend Terry Hearn for instance has probably landed the majority of his twenty-odd forties at this time. It is without question *the* best time for catching the biggies, and *the* time to go all out for that one fish. The carp will be getting ready for spawning any time now, certainly the most stressful time of their year, and it will be a period when they need to feed heavily to build up resistance to what lies ahead. They won't be too difficult to locate, usually heading to the areas where they expect to spawn, perhaps in the shallows where the water temperature will be ideal or close to weed beds and features that are going to offer protection to the eggs they deposit.

I went all out last year to catch the big mirror from Motorway Pond in East Yorkshire and, although that particular fish avoided me, I did land a number of other fine fish from the venue. This included four different thirties and a couple of 29lb mirrors, all of which came during May and June. I targeted one particular area of the lake, a section that was kind of midway between the shallows and the overwintering spots. The idea was to intercept the fish as they moved to spawn in late June.

I had a pre-baiting campaign in progress, which really helped keep the fish interested in the area I was targeting, baiting up quite heavily in between trips and then offering smaller traps when I was

My interception point at Motorway Pond in Spring 2005 during a heavy hail storm.

actually fishing. Carp are on the lookout for anything that resembles food in May, almost to the point that they become totally distracted from the danger that is present. Their need to build up stores of energy to get them through the rigours of spawning sees them eating quite a lot, with bites possible at any time of the day. At Motorway during this period of the year I was catching them at first light, lunchtime, tea-time, late evening and at midnight, as well as in the early hours. They were really onto the bait I was using and I had the rest of my strategy right, even to the point that I noticed that the fish were getting wise to my lines because they were getting choked up with suspended matter (I needed to clean them every few hours).

Pre-baiting always takes precedence at a water I am focusing on, but at other venues,

The second biggest resident in Motorway Pond, one known as The Long Fish, at 34lb 5oz.

The Stocking Bomb

I like to use a blend of different-sized pellets and particles, as well as some crushed boilies for my bombs. In the spring time, bright-orange Rod Hutchinson Scopex or yellow pineapple-flavoured boilies work well.

About three full twists will be enough. It should be nicely compacted into a tight ball. Now form a loop so that you can tie a knot in the top to secure the contents. Tighten this loop down on the contents and trim.

Before emptying the bait into the tube, make sure that the stocking is knotted at the bottom end. Now pour in some bait, making sure that it is compacted down at the bottom.

The ideal is to form a very tight little bomb. You can compact it further by twisting the stocking just above the contents.

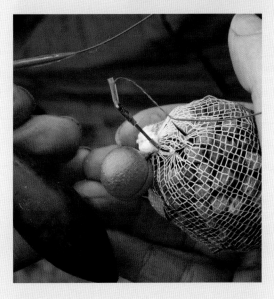

Slip the hook end of your rig securely through the mesh. It is now ready for casting.

such as those I might visit for a forty-eight-hour one-off trip, I use copious amounts of pellet to area-bait the swim. The pellet is there not to feed the carp up but to prolong their search for food. I really am into the idea that if a carp wants some food, knows there is some about but can't find it, it will be extremely easy to catch. This is one of the great things about pellet and, used like this, I regard it as an attractor rather than a

Steve Briggs with a spring-caught Colne Valley near-forty – the biggest fish in the lake.

PVA, which means that the lead can plummet out of sight into silt leaving just the lighter contents and hookbait in obvious positions. As a result, the bomb method lends itself well to critically balanced baits and pop-ups of about an inch or two. The hookbait is merely clipped onto the side of the bomb and then cast out. This dead simple tactic is ideal for waters that are quite heavily stocked. You can even tie a few bombs up at home, something that is done by a lot of the lads who fish in the very popular carp competitions, such as the British Carp Angling Championships.

Spring Progression

As spring nears an end everything will be lush and green lakeside and the fish will be closer to spawning. The rain and warmth from the sun will have established the weed beds around the lake, turned the lily beds into havens for the carp, and the reeds into tall thick vegetation clogged with colonies of snails and crustaceans, which the carp will love to spend hours picking away at. By the middle of June, the water environment will be full of all sorts of different smells, and much of the carp's natural food will be found in dense populations. As a result I will turn to a tactic slightly different from the stocking bomb.

Although quite similar to the bomb in principle, the standard PVA bag has an important difference in that it allows me to use slightly more bait than a bomb as well as offer a liquid food source poured neat onto the contents. The bombs I use are rarely greater than the size of a ping-pong ball, but with the bag I aim to offer a pile of bait about the size of an apple. I also do away with the pellets and area-baiting when using these; instead I just fire the bag into position with no freebait around. This is where the liquid food source comes in, with a Sense Appeal or Amino Blend com-

food. Pellet spread liberally around a swim with a spod takes some effort to do, but when the fish get a scent for it they just don't give up, especially in May and June when their competitive instinct is naturally coming to the fore.

Within the pelleted area I fire all rods out using small traps, usually armed with the same pellet and some crushed boilies to try to stimulate their curiosity. I particularly like the stocking bombs here, especially for waters that have quite a soft bottom. I use Korda's Funnel Webb to make these, a brilliant product, which comes with a plastic funnel to help the angler form the all-important bomb. The great thing about this method is that it is very simple to use. The hookbait and lead are not locked inside the

The PVA Bag Trap

For making the PVA bag trap, I use the Kryston Melt-Ex bags the most, although I must say that I like the new Fishrite ones with the draw cord at the top. The procedure I use for making the trap is as follows:

1. Place the hookbait only into the bag, pushing it into one of the bottom corners all by itself.
2. Then cover the hookbait with some whole or crushed boilies, filling the bag to about half full.
3. The lead is the last thing to go in. Rest this on top of the filling, ensuring that the hooklink is in a loop and isn't going to be obstructed by anything.
4. Then pour on the liquid food source, ensuring that the contents are given a good covering.
5. Next pack the bag down as neatly and tightly as possible, sealing it by folding down the top corners so that only the main line sticks out of the top. (To keep the top corners in place, I lick them and tightly wrap them around the bag.) Then leave it to stand for a few seconds before use.

I much prefer my hookbait to sit on top of the lead and the feed when it reaches the bottom, which is why I place it into the bag first. The bag will obviously fall through the water weight end down, the freebaits covering the lead and then the hookbait resting right on top in pole position. Another way I present my bags involves tying some PVA tape or string around the neck of the bag and then trimming the excess off. This gives

Packed and ready for launch!

the bag a lot more strength than the lick-and-stick method, which realistically can be used up only to about 70–80yd (65–75m). With the tie method, you can get a bag out in excess of 120yd (90m) comfortably, but obviously the bigger it is the more resistance there will be, so some modification to the size may be necessary depending on conditions on the day and how far out the fish are showing.

pound pushing a 'protein message' out to the fish rather than just the attraction that the pellets would provide.

This is an important change to the strategy because protein is the essential building block for carp and, with spawning about to take place at any moment, I'm convinced they are more sensitive to the difference between food and attraction at this time of the year than they are at any other.

JULY AND AUGUST

Post-Spawning Analysis

Come July, the summer will be in full swing and the carp in your target water are likely to have completed their first spawn of the year. This is the time when everything you've learnt in the spring is likely to change, because the effects of spawning really will deliver a serious change to the fishes' mood and patterns of behaviour. You will just about have got them sussed, to the point where you can almost set your clock to the moment you'll have a take, and now you can guarantee that everything will change. As an example, for the most part of last spring the carp at Motorway

Pond were really into an early-morning and midday feed. Any time between 5 a.m. and 9 a.m. was a great time, as indeed was 12.30–2.30 p.m., but by July – when they had finished their only spawn of the year – everything went out of sync. The angling pressure on the lake hadn't changed much from when I started fishing there earlier in the year, with fairly even pressure in the middle part of the week ranging up to heavy pressure at the weekends. There was a good supply of bait going in, too, but instead of there being a number of feeding periods in the day, there was now only one and that was right in the middle of the night. The carp were also being found in some really strange areas of the lake, parts that had been completely devoid of carp before spawning time.

Midsummer. Hot, sticky and not a great time for fishing with static baits.

You would expect the carp to be desperate to repair damaged tissue after a spawn, but at the majority of lakes I've fished it has been quite the opposite: the carp are in an almost semi-dormant state for anything up to two weeks afterwards. Spawning will have taken so much energy out of them that they won't even be interested in any pre-bait you offer them. They won't spook as easily as they do prior to a spawn and they certainly won't be as active. Generally I have a week's rest from a water when they have been spawning, visiting only to keep the pre-bait going in and to keep an eye on where they are resting up. The pre-bait is reduced to smaller amounts, and my return with the rods happens only once I know they have moved from the areas they have been resting in. I then begin with the same PVA bag approach I mentioned in June, focusing on the 'protein message' and the liquid additives, dropping it completely in favour of the pre-bait only once I know they are feeding stronger. I then stick with the pre-bait on the bottom all the way through the middle of summer, with a lot of days focused on stalking, a method of carping that I really do enjoy. Nothing quite beats getting up close and personal with a big fish, especially if the weather is hot and sticky and not very conducive to fishing with static baits.

Scratching Time!

Being a warm month of the calendar year, August usually sees the carp in the upper layers quite a lot, especially around midday

Early morning in July and the carp are spawning heavily in the weed.

There's nothing quite the same as getting up close and personal with a big carp, especially if the bottom baits are proving slow.

and during the afternoon and early part of the evening. I touched on the basics of stalking in *Discover Carp Fishing* with Rob, so I won't go over old ground here. Instead, I shall recall some observations I recently made during a week-long session in the UK while chasing after some hard-fished-for carp on the surface amongst a set of lily pads. There were fish in the lily bed for most of the week. I visited each day, firing out Mixers to see if there were any bigger fish present. I had a great chance to observe them because the bottom bait fishing was so slow; I spent long periods of time just watching and seeing if I could suss them out.

The carp very quickly homed in on the Mixers that I fired out at the start of each day. From the first handful I introduced, they fed very confidently on them, with two or three fish coming to the baits within five minutes. They really were searching for more as they confidently consumed one after another, and to be honest my

Even the sound of Mixer hitting the surface can attract fish.

adrenaline was rushing because they looked very susceptible to capture. They seemed to be feeding in a pattern. They would home in on the Mixer, take a couple, and then move off for a few minutes, apparently working in a rota and making sure they each got a piece of the action.

Their awareness of danger only started to develop when I fired out the hookbait. They knew something wasn't quite right from the off, as though they recognized the sound that the rig made as it hit the surface. From then onwards they were a lot more cautious, and as soon as one spooked on the hookbait they all disappeared for a long period of time, perhaps half an hour or so. During the week I tried all manner of different hookbaits, including cork, imitation Mixer, bread as well as glued-on Mixer. They really didn't like the imitation Mixer for some reason. They wouldn't even head in the direction of it, let alone look as if they were going to sample it. They responded to the cork the best, but seemed to reject it at the last minute as though something was not quite right with the presentation.

I started off by fishing with a standard controller set up with the line going across the surface, but after several rejections and no success I concluded that the reason they kept rejecting the cork hookbait wasn't my hook set-up, but rather that they were regulating their suction to single out the danger baits. As they homed in on the cork, they ever so gently sucked at it from underneath. I could see all of this very clearly because I was less than a rod length away from them. Even when I hid the line across the side of a lily pad, with the bait just on the edge, the fish didn't like it. I also noted several fish coming into the vicinity of the hookbaits, causing a bit of commotion so as to free all of the Mixers from around a pad, and then only sample the ones that looked as though they were not fixed to something.

They were very cute, and at the same time as discovering this I also decided to disguise the line by dapping the hookbait over the stem of a lily.

Surface Strategy

I eventually caught on my fourth day of studying them, by which time I think I had a good insight into their behaviour. I opted for pre-soaked Mixer on the hook, which I had prepared the night before. I just poured some scalding hot water on the Mixers, left them to soak for a minute and then strained all of the water off. I then left the soaked Mixers in a sealed tub overnight.

Despite having several rejections on the dapping method to start with, I persevered

Using a lot of surface bait is a great way to stimulate competition, especially if you introduce it little and often.

They wanted it that much they were even venturing out of the pads to sample.

two pre-soaked Mixers on the hook

Close-up on the hookbait.

with it, blaming the eliminations on the set-up I had chosen rather than the method. I would try to overcome the way in which the fish selected the hookbait using their suction by offering two Mixers on the hook. These would have to sit exactly right on the surface though. The idea was that the two together would be too irresistible and the fish wouldn't know how much suction would be needed to consume them because they were taking one at a time. Also, by having two Mixers on the hook, I could float the hook above them and allow some slack line between the bait and the lily stem the line was hung over. With only one Mixer on the hook, I needed to have the line fairly tight so that it didn't sink – resulting in no give when the fish sucked.

I placed the hookbait underneath the closest lily pad, with the line draped over the nearest stem and with about 2in (5cm) of give. This would help to make the bait more obvious to the fish and also over-come any shyness (they seemed to prefer the baits under the leaves). I also flavoured it with Solutein instead of leaving it natu-ral. A few other lads had been fishing for the carp on the surface and I knew the fish would respond better to something a little bit new. This was the first time I'd used the Solutein (a soluble form of Betaine) as an addition to Mixers, but I was confident it would get them dropping their guard.

To sum it all up, on the last day of my trip I caught one of the venue's biggest res-idents. I had a lot more fish in the swim – mainly, I think, down to the Solutein more than anything. I think the new smell brought the baits to the attention of more fish, which also stimulated competition amongst them, which in turn brought more to investigate. I fed them for about an hour before I cast in, building their confidence up to a catchable level. There was more than one fish really taking con-fidently, which was what I had aimed for

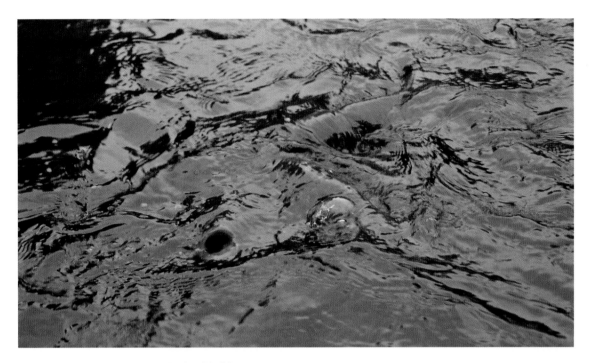

Feeding frenzy and time for the hookbait!

because I knew this would promote rivalry amongst them. After an hour, I could have had a couple of fish, but they weren't of the size I wanted so I lifted the hookbait away from them.

Eventually I managed to single out a biggie I wanted. It came really close in and took a couple of Mixers very confidently at my feet, which gave me a good glimpse of its size. I'd actually cast the hookbait out a long while before I saw the fish, leaving it draped over a lily stem until the time for me to lower it in arrived. When the big mirror was feeding strongly in the vicinity of the hookbait, I lowered it in and, less than a minute later, Bang! – it took it first time. There was nothing finicky about the take, a sign I had them sussed, and I watched the hook and Mixer disappear while a load of line shot across the surface and the battle commenced. It was an amazing climax to a long trip of watching,

trying and thinking. As it turned out, it was a personal best surface-caught UK carp of 29lb, a capture that goes to show that even in the thick of summer when not much is happening on the bottom, you can make things work in your favour.

SEPTEMBER AND OCTOBER

Early Autumn 'Hot Spots'

The need for plumbing and searching out the 'hot spots' becomes more obvious in early autumn than at any other time of the year. Generally speaking, results can be a bit hit and miss in September/October because the fish in your target venue are likely to have been bombarded with hoards of baited rigs in the preceding months. Yet if you track down the spots they visit regularly, you can certainly sneak a few chances before they really get their heads down when the big winds of November arrive.

Obviously a well-planned pre-baiting campaign will help overcome any shyness built up by the carp, but a good plumb around now will uncover all sorts of otherwise hidden areas, especially those that are generally termed by the carp angling fraternity as 'cleaned areas'. These areas of the lake bed may be only a few feet across, but as the weed density drops off with the cooler water, such hot spots can be uncovered fairly easily. Some weeds take much longer to die off than others, but one type that

The perseverance was well worth it. A new UK surface-caught personal-best mirror.

First signs of autumn.

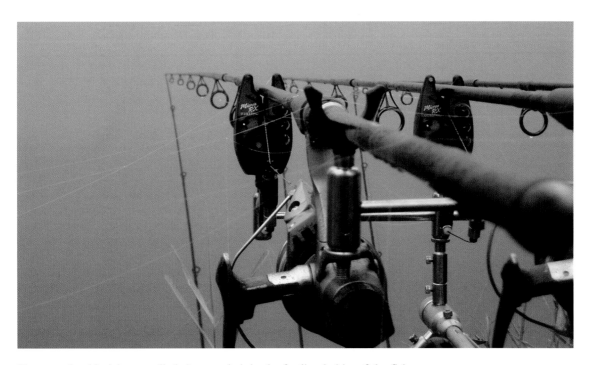

Damp and cold nights usually bring a switch in the feeding habits of the fish.

tends to go much quicker than most is the cotton-wool algae. Algae is present in all fisheries, but come the end of September or early part of October, blooms tend to lose their green colour and die back, taking on a darker appearance and making lake-bed examination a lot easier. Where cotton-wool blooms have been present during the summer, you tend to get a light coating of black fluff that resembles hair and can easily be picked up by the marker rod or lead. A smooth 'cleaned' piece of bottom is what I look for, and usually one that is at least a yard or so across and surrounded by black fluffy algae.

One of the best ways of uncovering cleaned areas is with a boat and some sort of looking glass, but not all venues allow anglers to do this, in which case it is necessary to have a good cast around. I use two

The best way of finding out what the bottom is really like is by checking the hook.

rods to do it thoroughly, the first armed with a simple marker float set-up, and the second loaded with a baited rig. I simply cast the marker out to the area I want to check, and then follow it with the rigged rod, taking note of anything I bring back on the hook. I cast all around the marker, giving the rig plenty of time to settle on the bottom, before retrieving it and moving my attention to another area.

Marking Territory

Since a cleaned area may well have been created by the feeding activities of the fish, the uncovering of one might mean you are on to a winner, but another suggestion offered by anglers is that these areas are 'cleaning spots': areas where the carp have rubbed themselves to dislodge any parasites and 'cling-ons' they may have picked up during the warmer weather.

I think the latter suggestion is a little bit misleading because I follow the line of thought that carp 'clean' themselves on the bottom in the early part of spring, ridding themselves of the parasites that have taken hold in the winter. Their day-to-day activity in the warmer weather tends to keep most parasites at bay, with any rubbing on the bottom in the early part of autumn being done as a form of marking territory rather than anything else. As the food stocks deplete, the fish become more aggressive towards each other, and their marking of territory is a survival instinct. As in the spring, this time of the year usually sees carp covered in red marks caused by such rubbing or, in clay pits, covered with clay markings down the side. The marks won't be as pronounced as they are after spawning, but nevertheless they will be obvious to the angler.

Despite the fish all thinking that 'cleaned' spots are their own, it is not unusual for these areas to produce multiple captures if you get things right. Your presentation will usually be spot on because the bottom is clean, with the next important part of the equation being the choice of the right tactics.

Agitated and Competitive

Early autumn is a time when the carp begin to group up. They start to get agitated and competitive. They know winter is on its way

An early-morning autumn mirror displaying marks on the flanks.

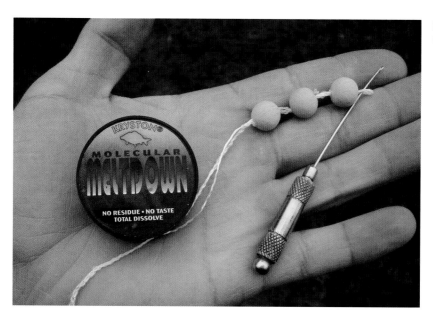

Stringers are an ideal early-autumn tactic.

and they head towards the areas they mark as their own and where they know there will be food. Such 'hot spots' are there waiting to be found by the angler. They may take some time to uncover, and they may be very isolated when you discover them, but early autumn is a transition time when the results generally come only to those who get each piece of the jigsaw right.

My own experiences very much point towards first tracking down the hot spots and then keeping the baiting levels fairly light. Half a dozen or so freebies on a stringer alongside the hookbait would be my first choice, perhaps with a light coating of pellet just to increase the attraction. I always find mimicking nature is the best option, which is why I like to keep everything as tight as possible (similar to the way the fish find bloodworm beds). Early autumn hot spots tend to be quite isolated, so there's no need for heavy or broad scatterings of bait just yet: these will come into their own towards the end of October, perhaps leading into November, when the weather changes and the fish get into their pre-winter feeding mode.

If you have been targeting a venue with the same bait throughout the season then no doubt you will have lost a bit of faith in it during August and September as the catches dropped off. This is the nature of carp fishing, but my advice is to have confidence in your hard efforts because now is the time that they will really show through. The carp will recognize an established bait now more so than at any other time of the year. To give you an example, in 2005 I'd been piling Hutchy's MC Addicted into the Motorway Pond since April and, despite having a rough couple of weeks fishing in August/early September, things picked up again for me in September. It had been hard listening to the advice from my friends that my target fish wasn't 'on' my pre-baited bait, but the capture of new fish certainly boosted my confidence that sticking with it was the right choice.

The Autumn Feed

As the season moves into October, the weather will take a turn for the worse with heavy rain, sleet storms and big winds.

With the overcast conditions will come a switch in the feeding habits of the carp as they recognize the onset of winter. A look back in history will identify that autumn is one of the best times for catching big carp, perhaps not quite as good as spring, but certainly the next in line. The back end of October, especially, sparks a lot of very strong winds from the west and south. Really strong, sometimes gale force at times, but conditions that really do stir up the bottom and get the carp rooting around. I know some waters don't respond well to big winds, but even though it can be very uncomfortable I've had a heck of a lot of great catches while fishing into them. I had some superb results fishing in the Top Dug Out swim at Orchid Lake a few years back, and I can say that if it's late October when you are reading this I'm likely to be out on the bank, preferably on one of the north or eastern sections of my target venue where the westerly and southerly winds will be hacking in.

With autumn also comes a lot of fallen leaves, which can cause one or two problems with your presentation if you don't take enough care. Even when fishing over my pre-bait I will completely switch to pop-ups at this time of the year, not wishing to

Here comes the wind and a change in the weather.

Double pop-up overshotted, ideal for combating fallen leaf matter.

risk having my hookbait hidden away underneath an obstruction. An inch or so off the bottom is what I go for when presenting a bait in this way, usually critically balanced, but occasionally overshot, especially if I'm in shallow water and there is an undertow. Generally I shorten my hooklinks for pop-ups, usually down to 6–8in (15–20cm). I think carp, especially pressured ones, tend to approach pop-ups by almost placing their mouths right over the top of the bait rather than hoovering up. A shorter link gives them less margin for error here, especially when combined with a heavy lead of, say, 4 to 5 ounces.

If ever there was a time when you need to have a good supply of bait in store, this is it. Autumn is the big feeding period of the year and, if you wonder how much bait a carp can feed on in one sitting, put your experiments into motion now. A fish you caught a couple of weeks earlier may well weigh a few pounds heavier come the start of November. It truly is the second coming of the big fish months.

NOVEMBER AND DECEMBER

Heavy Baiter

The higher levels of oxygen present in bodies of water during winter makes it increasingly possible for the carp to eat more in one feed, and this may be reflected in the low numbers of repeat captures which occur during the cooler months around some of our fisheries. At this time of the year, the fish will know winter has arrived, and a single sitting of intense feeding, which fills them up, may last them a number of weeks. All of the carp in a particular lake will feed at much the same time because the environmental conditions will dictate this. This 'early winter feed' is a classic occurrence on many of the hard-fished English waters and, very often, there will be a forty-eight-hour period during late November when a lot of the big fish around the country get caught.

My preferred tactic with November big carp is to bait very heavily with smaller freebies such as hemp, pellets, and 8mm and 10mm boilies, fishing a big bait over the top alongside a light scattering of other big baits, say 10 per cent compared with the rest of the feed. The smaller carp will almost certainly be preoccupied with the small baits first, hopefully inciting the larger fish to hang around and sample the bigger baits. You will catch smaller fish on the big baits for sure: that is the nature of November because the carp get so hungry as winter

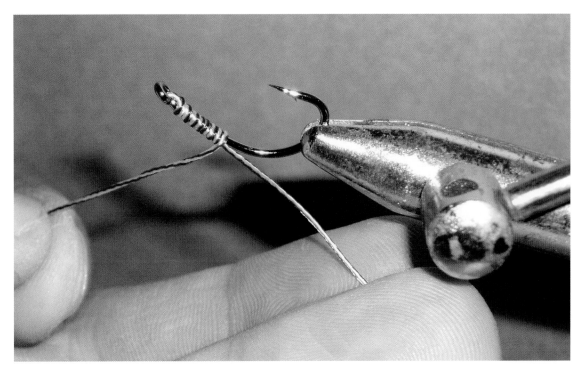

For pop-ups, I like the hair pivot coming off the back of the hook.

nears that they will feed heavily on everything. It is a working swim method when it comes to the big fish, as you are trying to stimulate competition but at the same time attract more fish into the swim. You will need to keep topping the swim up regularly after each fish, but as always the tactics that work best will be determined by the stocking density of the lake and its inhabitants.

Coldwater Feeding Patterns

Results wise, I'd say that winter has perhaps been my best time of the year to fish for carp. I've had a lot of good fish from November through to March from quite a few tricky waters, including several thirties from venues where a fish of that size is a nice result. I've never really been one for going to a lake just for a day session unless rules dictated that I had to or unless I was

going there with the intention of baiting up or walking around. However, if ever there was a time when day-only sessions are

November. Bring them to the feast!

I like to carpet-feed a swim with lots of small items, such as pellet and particle, along with small boilies to really get them rooting.

Darkness was a complete waste of time at Birch Grove in the winter, but the days were a different story altogether – as this 27lb 12oz common proves.

worth a try then in my experience the winter time is it. Fishing in the colder months of the year has produced so many fish for me during the day that for this coming winter I've already convinced myself that instead of sitting through the cold motionless nights when I just know nothing is going to happen, I'm going to try to be a bit more selective.

Everything is always going to be site-specific when it comes to identifying the feeding times of the carp because some venues have a higher stocking density than others, but I believe it to be more than just coincidence that most of the lakes I have fished in the winter have responded well

during the day. I recall Lee Jackson once writing a similar thing in a *Carpworld* article a couple of years back. When I fished on Birch Grove in the late 1990s and early part of this century, you could almost set your watch to the time when the fish would start feeding during the winter months. In my six years of being a member, off the top of my head I can think of only one fish that I caught in the hours of darkness during the months of November, December, January and February. I ended up with quite a few fish coming in the dark in March – when the water started to warm up a notch and the fish began waking up from winter dormancy – but during the thick end of the strong winds, frosts, rain and snow, it's almost safe to say that darkness was a complete waste of time.

A lot of the fish I caught from Birch came in two very distinct feeding spells, these being between 7 a.m. and 10 a.m. and then between midday and about 2.30 p.m. I can also recall similar results from other tricky waters I have fished in the winter. I consider Orchid Lake to be a similar kind of water to Birch when it comes to its difficulty level, and there I have also encountered mostly daytime action in the winter. Albeit slightly tougher, I noted the same at

A November near-thirty in a shower of sleet at first light.

Who would ever have predicted this – a winter carp at a tough venue taking Mixers off the surface?

the very tricky Dolly Mill fishery, which is owned by Rod Hutchinson. There are other examples too.

Exactly why carp choose their feeding times when they do no one knows for sure, but I suspect the more obvious reasons are to do with their levels and times of activity as well as their awareness of danger. In the scientific world carp are classed as diurnal feeders and said to be stimulated by the length of daylight available. I could set my watch by the action of the Motorway Pond carp in the early part of the season, but as

the year progressed I had to adjust things month by month. The spring differed from the summer, as did the autumn and early part of winter. During the summer I actually wrote a piece in *Carp-Talk* about my observations, changes that I know for sure were influenced by the regular and prolonged application of angling pressure.

One theory put forward for the consistency of daytime captures in winter is that this phenomenon may be the beginning of an annual cycle – or the end of it, depending on which way you look at it. Perhaps,

Bright single hookbaits, my favourite and most successful winter tactic.

when the activity of the carp begins to decline and the angling pressure drops off, they become increasingly aware of the shortening day and the reduction in the number of leads and lines around them. Perhaps their built-in body clocks begin to rule their feeding habits rather than their awareness of danger.

December Day Sessions

Learning the patterns of feeding of the carp at your target venue not only helps you to pick and choose when to fish a water, but it helps to get the tactics right on the day. I've always found another secret to success in the winter is getting the baits in place before the fish start to feed. I used to get myself up nice and early on Birch, getting things set in the dark so that the rods could be in place for daylight. A fresh pile of bait or freshly positioned hookbait I always find works better than one that has been left out overnight or for hours on end.

Whilst I've caught very well by casting baits right on top of showing fish in the winter, I must say that I don't like excessive casting around. I've found that you don't always need to be as spot on with your placement as you do, say, in the summer when the carp can be very finicky. A

cast that is within a few yards of where a fish has shown will usually be tracked down fairly quickly, since coldwater carp have a tendency to go looking for food when the time has arrived for them to replenish their energy levels.

This same line of thought is one of the reasons why I believe the tactic of scattering a few freebaits over a well-spread-out area also works well. My favourite December tactic is to use single bright-coloured (yellow or orange) hookbaits, critically balanced and fired out with no bag, stringer or bomb attached. Using the throwing stick I will then fire out between ten and twenty boilies in the vicinity, trying to get a fairly broad spread on them so that the fish have to go looking for them. Especially over deep silty areas this tactic has produced countless good results for me. It is as if the carp venture away from their holding areas to these parts of the lake on the lookout for any food items that are easy to access.

The water clarity is usually nice and clear in December, making anything on the bottom stand out to the fish, which is perhaps why bright-coloured hookbaits are so effective and are so often taken almost instantly. Deciding how many freebaits to fire out is a kind of balancing act really. You don't want so many that the fish fill them-

You've got to be out there doing it. Even in conditions like these there's still a chance.

selves up on them, but you do want sufficient to promote rooting around and the 'Oh, there's another one' syndrome. I tend to think that in the winter, when carp need to feed, they will expend quite a lot of energy on the search, scouring the lake bed if needs be, to the point that their need for food overpowers their instinct to be on their guard. I'm convinced this is one of the reasons why this month often sees some of the trickier fish in a lake make an appearance and also sees some truly outstanding captures for the anglers that are willing to brave the elements.

3 Underwater Carp Fishing

Over the years there have been many theories put forward by anglers on what happens below the water surface. In 2004 top tackle manufacturer Korda Developments released some DVDs of very eye-opening underwater footage: they showed carp approaching baited areas and even taking rigs in their mouths. Nothing, however, is quite the same as actually going under the water for yourself and having a good look around. One man who knows a thing or two about life below our lakes is my old mate Rob Hughes, a Sky Sports television presenter, very experienced carp angler

and fully qualified diver. Here's what he told me about his underwater observations at some of the carp lakes he's been fortunate enough to have had a real carp's-eye view of:

Simon   What made you want to take up diving?

Rob   I've always been a bit of a snorkeller, and passing my diving exam was something I always wanted to do. I had to take my PADI (Professional Association of Diving Instructors) exam before I could

The world below the surface, as a mid-twenty common swims past the camera in the St Lawrence river, USA.

Rob Hughes, a qualified diver, all kitted out for a plunge below the surface.

Park, Kingfisher Lake on the Bluebell complex, and also at the Cotswold Water Park.

Simon From the carp angler's perspective, which was the most interesting of the venues?

Rob They were all interesting and had something different about them. Kingsbury was a real eye-opener because it was the first time I actually interacted with carp. They came out of the snags I was swimming close to, and were inquisitive about this new arrival in their environment. They had a distinct interest in me, and the longer I stayed around their 'zones' the greater the numbers that came out to look. I'd even say that they were communicating with one another because the first fish I saw was a loner. It spooked when it first saw me, then returned with another fish, a bit like when you watch them feeding on baits. They'd come out and have a little look at me and then disappear, only to return with other fish. At one stage I had a dozen fish close to me in the deep bay area of the lake. It was incredible. Another interesting part of the dive at Kingsbury was that when I saw fish in open water, they bolted off, whereas when I saw them close to the holding areas like snags, they had much more confidence and stayed near to me.

Simon It must have been fairly clear down there. Did you see any signs of feeding areas?

Rob It was very clear at Kingsbury. The depth was around 7ft maximum and I could see very well. I came across a number of interesting areas on the bottom, which may have been feeding spots. I also saw some that I labelled scratching spots. The difference between the two was very obvious. In the 9 acres or so of water, I saw three different scratching spots all in the softer clay bottom.

do it, which I did in Malta, and ever since I passed I've been doing it wherever I've been allowed. As an angler, I can safely say that going under the water is much more revealing than dragging a lead and plumbing the depth!

Simon What high-profile carp fisheries have you dived in then?

Rob I've been in plenty of low-profile waters, but some of the high-profile ones include the St Lawrence river in the USA, Lac de St Cassien and Lac de Madine in France, Donaldson Dam in South Africa, and at home I've dived at Kingsbury Water

I labelled them scratching spots because the fish I saw swimming close by to them had clay markings down their flanks. I also saw the marks in the clay, which indicated they had been caused by the flanks of the fish rather than by their feeding activities. These spots were almost crater-like, about 8–12in deep and the size of a dustbin lid. They weren't perfect craters, but almost.

Simon They sound like the spots I've seen on the bottom at Tilery Lake. What was so different about these to those you labelled feeding areas?

Rob The craters may well have been feeding spots, full of bloodworm, which had been created by the foraging activities of the fish, but I labelled them scratching spots

because of the clay markings on the fish. It's hard for me to describe how different they were to those I termed feeding spots. You needed to see them for yourself. Basically, the feeding spots were over harder bottom and had quite obviously been picked at by the fish. There were small piles of stones that looked out of place, as though they had been moved there by something, and the bottom around them was almost polished clean. There's always a bit of dust on the bottom of all lakes, but these were spotless. They stood out very clearly from the rest of the lake bed, with strands of weed and bits of silt surrounding them. One interesting thing I noticed about these spots was that they were about the size of an A4 sheet of paper and were always in the middle of cleanish areas about the size of a table. They

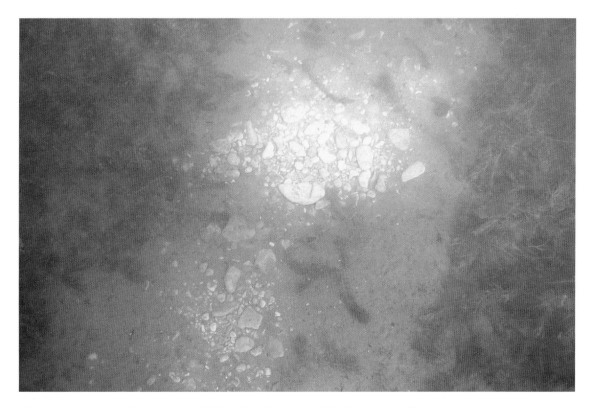

The feeding areas at Kingsbury had little piles of stones within clear areas of bottom.

weren't hollowed out like the clay scratching spots, just flat and very clean.

Simon   Tell us about diving at Cassien, a legendary venue the world over, and very different to your typical English water like Kingsbury.

Rob   Cassien is a very deep oligatrophic lake so there were lots of interesting things there. The deepest I went down to was 38ft. Even as far down as this I could see very easily for 13 to 16ft all around, so the theory amongst anglers about it being dark down there is nonsense. I went through several warm areas of water, too, not so much thermoclines – where a certain layer/depth of water is distinctly different to others – but rather isolated pockets of warmer and colder water. I think that because Cassien is quite an open lake that gets strong winds blowing, you probably don't get a thermocline forming there in the summer months

because it gets turned over so much by the chop and undertow.

Simon   Did you see any signs of fish feeding areas like those you saw at Kingsbury?

Rob   The typography is completely different so I didn't. The bottom is very rocky and difficult for the fish to dig up. However, I could see where the fish had been feeding, or picking on the bottom. Again, it's difficult to tell you what these spots were like, but I saw little trails in the light silt, a bit like when you see a sheep trail in a field, as if they had been created by more than one fish following one another. There's a lot of shoal fish at Cassien, so I'm presuming these trails were where their bellies had been mooching about on the bottom.

Simon   I know from having watched your TV series on Sky Sports [called *The Carp*

At Cassien there were little trails on the bottom where the fish had been mooching about.

Show] that you did some tests on casting while at Cassien. Can you tell us about those?

Rob They were really eye-opening. Because the venue has very good water clarity, Jon 'Shoes' Jones and I decided to do some tests: Jon stood on the bank with a rod in hand casting while I swam down to investigate how different rigs landed on the bottom. The conclusions we drew were that it certainly pays to feather a cast if you like your hooklink to lie flush to the bottom and away from the lead. If you didn't feather, every time you cast in, even

with a stiff rig, the hooklink concertinaed up on itself, especially with the supple braided links. The braided links basically wrapped themselves around the line, always tangling as if you were fishing with a chod rig with a very short hooklink length. Even when feathering the cast there were problems with this rig, and the best solution was to use a stringer and feathered cast combined, resulting in the link flattening itself out and lying much better on the bottom. We used various braided links in the tests and the one thing we observed with each brand – even when we tried to take the air bubbles out of

Putting his angling abilities to the test. Rob with a 48lb margin-caught mirror from Shropshire.

them (submerging and squeezing prior to casting) – is that they all floated, including those sold as sinking materials. One brand floated so much that it even pushed the pellets out of the way when we used it in a PVA bag.

Simon Tell us about the stiff rig tests.

Rob We found these to be much better at straightening out on the bottom, especially when feathered on the cast. They never fell exactly as we all expect them to though (with the bait coming to lie the length of the hooklink away from the lead), but they were distinctly better than the braids.

What we found with these was that it was best to tweak the lead ever so gently after casting out, just to straighten the link so that it wasn't so obvious. The stiffer the link, the better it would fall through the water, but the one thing I would always advise is to loop one end of the rig so that there is some movement in it. We also did some tests on combi-links. Some were terrible because the coating was so thin that they performed just like the braids in that they concertinaed on top of the lead.

Simon What type of hookbaits were you using in the tests and did you draw any conclusions from them?

In the weed at Cassien – simply the perfect lake to dive in with its crystal-clear water.

Rob We used all types, and we found that it was always better to use a lighter hookbait if you wanted it to kick away from the lead. A critically balanced bait on a really stiff rig was much better at coming to rest the length of the hooklink away from the lead, for obvious reasons (the lighter hookbait is easier to 'push' away from the rig).

Simon What about pop-ups and bottom baits?

Rob There's nothing much to say about them because the lighter a bait the better it gets 'pushed' away by the stiff link. One thing I can say about pop-ups is that the deeper you go in the water column, the greater the pressure applied to a bait. The more pressure there is, the more the air and flavour inside a bait is forced out. Basically, an air-compressed pop-up (one that is microwaved) used in shallow water will stay popped up for a longer period than one used in deeper water. If an angler is planning on fishing deep water, as many do at Cassien (some fish 100ft), I would advise using a pop-up made with a cork ball insert, especially if the angler plans on leaving the bait out overnight.

Simon Did you see any fish at Cassien?

Rob No I didn't, but one thing that was interesting is that on one day I got in the water to do some underwater filming while Rene Hawkins played a fish from a boat. We were waiting for this to happen so we were quick to react to the take and commence filming. As the fish neared the boat, it was very clear that it was trying to use me as a snag to help it free the line. At one time it swam right into me and I had to brush it and the line away with my hands. You can actually see it on the film that we shot in the TV series. The fish especially liked my snorkel, which was attached to my face

Note the fluorocarbon hooklink, which looks invisible.

mask and not in use. The line got wrapped up in it a couple of times.

Simon Let's consider the other waters you've dived at. Any other interesting observations to reveal?

Rob At the Cotswold Water Park, there were some interesting findings on weed and spodding. I was there with Brian Jarrett to make a film about the spod mixes he'd used in the British Carp Angling Championships to win the title for the second time with Dave Gawthorn. Firstly I'll say that whenever anglers spod up, we are never as accurate as we think we are, even if the spod is landing every time on the marker. Accuracy depends on how the spod falls through the water: this determines where the bait is deposited. If it bombs into the water, the bait starts to get deposited as the water is forced into it, making it leave an almost linear line of bait

69

A carp's-eye view of a combi-rig with a critically balanced bait.

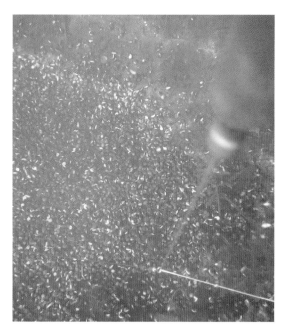

Exactly how accurate are we at baiting up with a spod? (Photo: Jon Jones)

rather than a nice tight clump as many would expect. You need to feather the spod on the cast to make it form the tighter clump.

Simon What did you find out about the weed?

Rob If a lake is quite weedy, it's likely there will be many channels in the weed, which we can't see from above. This is especially so with Canadian pondweed, which grows so well that it falls back on itself leaving little cubbyhole tunnels, which the fish use as route ways. They are like little mazes with hedges all around. Another interesting thing we found was that when Brian hooked a fish one time, it was solid his end, and he thought it had found a snag. I dived in with the camera to take a look and I could clearly see that the fish was ever so slightly in the weed, just up

Little trails in the weed created by the movement of the fish over the top.

to its gills. The way that the fish had put angles on the line took all of the leverage out of the rod so that at Brian's end it felt snagged. It was quite amazing.

Simon Any observations about sound underwater?

Rob It's difficult to tell which direction a sound comes from, but it can be heard four times more clearly than it can from above the surface. A cast can clearly be heard from under the water, as can bait falling in. One time I even heard a lead being dragged over some gravel. I also noted that high-pitched sounds from outside are easier to

hear than low tones, so if an angler is fishing very close in I would advise keeping the buzzers set on a low tone.

Simon Any other interesting points to tell us about?

Rob Another important thing worth mentioning relates to sight. When you look laterally in water it is harder to see than when positioned above something, such as when in a boat. You notice this more when you are filming because you need light to make a good picture. You don't get the same light refraction laterally as you do when looking down on something because

Back she goes – viewed from under the water.

the sunlight, which obviously comes from above, assists so much when doing this. Also, even when looking from above, it is much harder to make out darker areas of bottom, like weed or silt, whereas with lighter bottoms like gravel and sand it is much easier to see things. I'm sure this has an effect on the visibility of the rig to the fish. You can see a lot over the darker areas of bottom, but you can see much, much more over the lighter areas.

Simon Thanks for taking the time to talk to us. I'm sure there is something in what you have said that can aid all of us next time we are on the bank. Any chance you can come up to my local lakes and tell me where the feeding spots are ...?

4 Bait-Boat Carping

Love 'em or loath 'em, there's no denying that bait boats represent a substantial part of the modern-day carp scene. Not every venue allows their use, but certainly a large proportion of carp anglers use them where they can. I fall into the category of user, and over the years bait boats have caught me a fair number of carp that I perhaps wouldn't have caught without their assistance.

To a lot of the non-users bait boats are categorized as a form of cheating because they are 'easy to use' and a substitute used by anglers that 'can't cast'. All I can say to these comments is, how many of the critics have actually used one? I won't deny that once you get the hang of using a boat they do make the bait placement side of things very easy, but there is still an element of

It isn't a case of just load one up and away you go: there's much more to a bait boat than meets the eye.

Be realistic about the range at which you use a bait boat. Don't upset or interfere with other anglers.

the users laugh. With today's boats you can bait tight, heavy, sparse, broad, or however you like. There is even a boat on the market in Holland, sold by Tony Schrijver (Schrijver Bait Boats), that allows us to place freebaits out individually, so forget the idea that all bait-boat users use them in the same way.

Most boats take a fair bit of getting used to, but when you are dropping the baits out with ease you may discover more water to fish, especially if there are certain areas of your target lake that tend not to be fished much because of restricted casting. The range you can use a boat at depends on the type you buy, but most of the newer models are claimed to operate well up to a range of about 600yd/550m (athough why someone would need to use one at that range is beyond me – at that sort of distance you really are straining your eyes to see it clearly, even with binoculars, and, more to the point, they can be hard to manoeuvre at that distance too). I myself have used one at about 400yd (370m), but one thing I have found is that you really do need to make for some higher ground if you want 'real time' operation. Over 300yd (270m) I have experienced interference at certain venues, with the boat going off in the opposite direction to the way I want it to go, as well as the hopper opening up when I've not triggered it! Even at shorter distances I have experienced similar interference so my advice is be realistic about the range you use your boat at.

As for operation, most boats have one style of steering on the handset, with a forwards and backwards on one joystick and a left and right steering on another stick. In recent years I have seen some boats, especially those with two jets, that operate in a different way. With these, each joystick will operate each jet, meaning that you have to push them both forwards or backwards to make each jet power, and to make

skill in using one in a successful way. After almost ten years of having a boat, I for one certainly don't just press a button and away I go. I can also cast very efficiently, too, so it really is inaccurate to brandish all users as 'non-casters'.

The obvious reason why most people use a bait boat is that it allows anglers the chance to place their hookbait and freebait out in one very simple operation. There's no need to thrash the water to a foam when using a bait boat. There's no need for re-baiting after leaving a bait hanging in the trees either, because that just doesn't happen if you know what you are doing. As for the theory that bait boats offer only one form of presentation, well that just makes

A closer look at the type of controls you should expect on a standard handset.

You'll need a good weed-guard on the jets/pumps if you don't want to run into any problems, especially if you are fishing a weedy water. This is the guard on a propeller-powered Blue Sky Angling Lake Star boat.

it turn you have to balance it exactly right. Personally I find this operation slightly more difficult than the other but, like anything, with time it becomes easier.

Usually one joystick, or the left and right setting on the newer handsets, trigger the lights on the boat as well as the hopper release, but you may find different operations with different designs. Certainly those from Angling Technics differ from those sold by Viper.

WHICH BOAT?

The first item I would want is a weed-guard on the bottom of the boat. Some boats operate using pumps whilst others have propellers. With both forms, you need a guard of some description because you will be forever losing your boat in the mid-

dle of the lake in summer when the weed is high. A lot of the modern-day designs have a weed-guard as standard, but certainly in some of the early models they were non-existent, so if you are buying second-hand make sure you ask the relevent questions before you agree to buy.

The amount of bait the boat can carry will be a deciding factor in what you can do with it. With those whose bait-carrying capacity is low, you will have to keep running it out to get the baiting situation you require, which will result in more battery drainage. The bigger the boat, the larger the compartments for bait are likely to be. I would want a boat that can carry a minimum of 1kg. If you consider 1kg of boilies in 18mm size, that would perhaps equate to (and I'm guessing here) 200 freebaits. A smaller-sized bait would obviously offer you more, but 200 × 18mm would give you

The weed-guard on the jet-powered Viper.

The Microcat, with its two battery compartments, is ideal for choppy conditions.

a lot of scope if you needed to bait that heavily with large baits.

In my experience, having two hoppers on a boat does not give a user much of an advantage capacity-wise because, in some cases, one single hopper can be loaded with the same amount of bait that two can carry, even though the size of them looks substantially different. The only advantage of having two hoppers is they allow you to place the hookbait to the side of a baited area. I've tried taking two lines out (one in each hopper), but if you are fishing any-where over about 30yd (25m) range you will just run into problems. The lines will become entangled and it really is more hassle than it's worth if you ask me.

The weight of a boat is important for several reasons. The first is obviously car-riage. If you need to walk a fair distance to your swim then a heavy boat will restrict the amount you can carry in one go. However, a heavy boat tends to sit better in the water than the lighter models and is therefore much better in choppy condi-

tions. The Microcat from Angling Technics operates with two batteries and is therefore very heavy, but it is by far the best boat for choppy conditions I have used. On Tilery Lake in East Yorkshire the wind can soon turn the water into waves, but the Microcat really does handle them well – cutting through them with ease. There are battery compartments each side of this boat, which aids balance, but the one thing you will have to do before sending it out is ensure that they are taped up. Water can easily slip down the sides of these compartments as it laps over the side.

While the Microcat is by far the best for big waters and choppy conditions, the one thing I will say about the Viper model is that it is the best all-rounder I have used. It is a fairly lightweight boat, carries a lot of bait, can be used at long range, is easy to use, has very visible lights, and basically needs no add-ons. I have used this boat in very choppy water and, though not as good as the Microcat for this, it can deal with all but the worst conditions fairly well. The

You'll need to tape over the battery compartments of a Microcat to stop water from weighing the boat down.

only really negative thing I can say about this boat is that the blue LEDs on the back are too bright. I've noticed this on the Microcat as well, but at least with the Viper it has a concentrated ring of white LEDs at the front, which helps; the Microcat has only two very low-powered white ones that you can hardly make out. The back blue ones can blur out on you on a misty night, which can sometimes get you confused as to the direction the boat is going. A good tip is to place a dot on each LED with a black permanent marker pen, which does lighten them somewhat.

BAIT-BOAT TOOLS

Something I have found since I started using boats is that the more add-ons you need, the more hassle and expense it will mean in the long run. I would advise someone buying a boat for the first time to go for one that has everything included with it. When you purchase a standard bait-boat kit you will more than likely get the boat, handset, chargers for the batteries and the batteries themselves included. Most boats come equipped with LEDs on the front, sides and back so that you can see them in the dark (red and green at the sides), and all come with aerials. There are loads of other tools that you can buy to upgrade your boat, depending on how much you want to spend. If you want some extra lights on the front and back these are available. If you want extendable aerials for extreme-range fishing you can get these. The same goes for floppy aerials so you can get right underneath overhanging bushes without getting the boat stuck.

The best item of gear I have come across that is well worth paying extra for is the remote echo-sounder. You can buy various sorts, ranging from a standard depth-finder to a graphical one. The standard depth-finders will measure depths down to 165ft (50m) and have a range of 220yd (200m). These are absolutely ideal for all kinds of fishing and the best I have used is by Angling Technics. The software they use contains DSP (digital signal processing), which uses smart averaging algorithms to give an accurate record. I also understand that Eric's Angling Centre in Leeds is now offering a service whereby they can fit a Smart Cast type depth-finder to a boat, which may come in useful if you don't want to pay top money for a branded name design. Although I've never used one of these, I'm sure the shop will be able to offer you some excellent advice on them.

If you really want to push the boat out though, there is nothing better than a graphical echo-sounder. This will give you

a visual account of what is below the boat rather than just a depth reading. The Viper uses a Garmin Fishfinder 100. I'm unsure of its exact depth range, but I once managed to get a reading from 50ft (15m) at one of my local pits when I first tried it out. I've also seen one of my German friends using a Garmin 100 (not in a remote boat) at Cassien where depths range to 150ft (45m). The Viper operates its graphic sonar by using a standard portable television connected to a beam receiver that sits on the bank. This is a bit fiddly in comparison to the Microcat one, which uses a Fulcrun Design that incorporates advanced DSP. This picks up the beam using a hand-held receiver that also has the graphics built in.

Despite the awkwardness with the Viper it gives me a lot of confidence knowing that

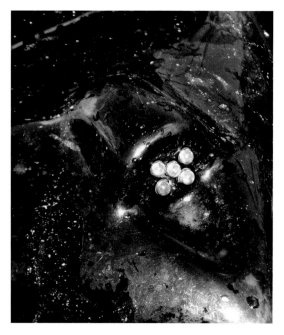

Bright LEDs make all the difference for night-time navigation.

The hand-held depth-reader by Angling Technics. They also sell a hand-held graphic sounder.

The Garmin fish-finder inside the Viper. Easily the most accurate of the sounders available.

I am using a sounder that has not been specially made for a bait boat. The Garmin Fishfinder 100 that it uses has a grey line facility as well as all of the standard depth and fish-finding abilities. The grey line enables you to identify how hard the bottom is below the boat, allowing you to find soft silty areas or hard gravel patches. I'm not knocking any of the purpose-made remote-control boat sounders here but, having been brought up on the Garmin and Eagle type for use on the big waters in a rowing/engine-sized boat, at least I am confident that the signal is very accurate. I am also confident that the beam receiver that it uses works closer to 'real time' than other models.

There are loads of other tools that you may come across in tackle shops or on websites, but the only other items I would advise anyone to get are a protective carry bag and some spare batteries. Bait boats are extremely fragile and they have a habit of malfunctioning if they are not looked after.

My friend Derek Fell calls his boat his little egg, and I wouldn't disagree. Drop it and you'll almost certainly need to send it back. Treat it like an egg, and keep it well protected, and you won't go far wrong.

As for spare batteries, these are essential items of kit, especially when you are at a big water where you need to run the boat out well over 100yd (90m) each time. Obviously distances like this are a big drain on the power source, so it pays to have at least one replacement set for the handset and boat wherever you go. The handset used for both the Microcat and the Viper is pretty much the same in that you can get two or three days of regular use before it begins to drain down (unlike the boat, which will more than likely be flat a lot sooner). The batteries used in the boats are the 12-volt type used for burglar alarms. The Microcat runs on two of these, and since they aren't light they help it to sit low in the water, giving excellent stability. The Viper contains only one battery.

You can buy a recharger that works on a solar panel, which enables you to maintain power while on the bank, but even on a bright sunny day these are not up to charging batteries from flat to full power. They are purely a means of trickle charge, so it is always wise to get hold of a few spare batteries.

THOUGHTS ON PRESENTATION

An awful lot of big fish tend to get caught by anglers using bait boats, especially on waters where they are not used very often, or perhaps used by only a small percentage of the

A bait-boat-assisted 32lb November-caught mirror. What a stunning fish!

anglers. One of the reasons for this is almost certainly that the anglers are using a boat with two hoppers, allowing the angler to drop each hopper simultaneously to gain an advantage on the presentation side of things.

There is an old saying in carp fishing that the big carp tend to hang around the baited area on the outside. They are usually perceived to be the older and much more wary fish, which will confront an area of bait with a certain amount of caution. OK, there are exceptions to this rule, but I think you will understand the theory I am trying to describe here. By filling one hopper on the boat with all of the free offerings and the other with just the hookbait, you can accurately place the hookbait right on the edge of the bait and therefore in a good position for catching the bigger fish. It doesn't always work, but I am sure that this presentation does lend itself well to waters where boats are not used a lot or indeed where this method of presentation is not used very much.

A heavy bed of pellets and particles in the one hopper with a largish-size hookbait in the other has worked well for me and some of my friends who use boats regularly, but there are of course other options depending on the type of water you are fishing and what the fish within it have been subjected to. The only thing you have to be careful with when using this presentation is not to overload the one side of the boat with bait when there are strong winds. As soon as you release the heavy side (full of bait), the boat will rock violently, and in a good chop it may even capsize – even if the boat's design is otherwise very stable.

Using PVA in the Boat

Why use PVA bags in a boat some of you may wonder? Especially since the boat will drop all of your baits in a nice tight clump once you open the hopper. Well, on waters that are fairly deep or very weedy, where you want a much more concentrated area of bait, a PVA bag on the bottom may be just the answer. The difficulty with using PVA in a bait boat is keeping it dry until you want to drop it. Some boats are so low in the water they are useless for PVA presentations. Their hoppers run so low to the water surface that they take on board water through the door openings. The Microcat is a boat that I would not recommend for PVA because it is designed to sit very low, to enhance stability, whereas the Lakestar by Blue Sky Angling has a hopper that sits a lot higher and is much better.

When using bags I first load the hopper with pellets or boilies, enough to give the whole of the base a covering. If any water does come from underneath the boat it is likely to be in the splash form only, so this covering ensures the bag has a cushion to lie on. Double bagging obviously gives the presentation extra armour too.

It is possible also to get splash from overhead, so to keep this area protected I cover it with electrical tape. The 2in (5cm) wide type is the best, and I carry a roll with me at all times. It is one of the essential bait-boat pieces of kit. Even in a light wind it is possible to get splashes over the top of the boat as it runs into waves so it pays to keep the top as sheltered as you can. All I do with the tape is cover the whole of the surface of the hopper. This is another reason why the Viper is such a good-all round boat: the hopper is very deep and there is no chance of the PVA sticking to the underneath of the tape.

The use of PVA in carp fishing today is so essential that I really am amazed that bait-boat manufacturers have not looked at designing a specific mechanism for protecting a presentation. As it is, no bait-boat company has yet made a boat with a hopper lid as well as an underneath cushion of some sort. I am sure that with a bit of

When using PVA bags, first load the hopper with pellets or boilies, enough to give the whole of the base a covering.

Now cover the top of the hopper with tape to keep the PVA bag dry.

thought a whizz-kid could come up with a boat design that dispenses with the need for my tape method, which is so time-consuming. I am also sure that such a boat would sell like hot cakes.

Single Hookbaits

I have had a lot of success using my boat with a single hookbait presentation, especially on waters where boats are used a lot. A few years ago I caught fairly well on the Motorway Pond doing this and, in more recent times, I have also taken some nice fish from Tilery Lake. Most bait-boat users tend to place an amount of bait into the boat alongside the hookbait. It's almost an obsession: they have to put something in or it's not right. After extensive use, the carp are sure to get wise to any presentation, so overcoming their shyness demands a little bit of thought. Using a single hookbait in a boat takes a bit of getting used to but, believe me, it does work very well if you can get your head around trying it.

5 With a Bit of Help From a Boat ...

The advantages boats offer the carp angler are so great that they are now a common piece of kit for many anglers, especially those who fish the likes of Wraysbury, Fen Drayton or any of the overseas waters. The first thing I will always say to anyone wishing to purchase a boat for the first time is, what do you need it for? Transporting you? Transporting your gear? Or both? Most of the time, we could all do with one

Boats are now an essential item of kit at some UK venues, including Wraysbury – the home of the former British record.

Zodiac make some of the best boats on the market.

that is good enough for both tasks, but if you are into the long-session type fishing, which I and a lot of my friends are, then you will certainly need one for both.

I have two inflatables, but they are so different from each other that they need some explanation. One is made from a lightweight PVC-type material; the other is made from canvas. The canvas one has a wooden floor, while the PVC one has only an inflatable floor. This is the first important point to consider when buying a boat because if you are going to be transporting yourself over any sort of distance, you will need one that has a rigid floor. For a gear boat, a rigid floor is not really essential because most of the weight will be spread over a large area. Obviously, a plastic or fibreglass boat would be an excellent choice, but then you would have to consider their ease of carriage. I have an estate car, which has plenty of space into which I can fit all of my gear as well as the boats folded down. I much prefer to have a boat inside the car than to have it on the roof as it's much easier on the fuel consumption.

There isn't a great deal of difference between the prices of inflatables and plastic or fibreglass boats. For a brand new boat that I would recommend as suitable for carp fishing purposes, you would be looking at a price somewhere in the region of what it would cost to buy a high-quality washing machine. Some will obviously be a lot more than this, as it all depends on what sort of gadgets and size you want. Forget all the labels indicating that a boat is four-man, two-man or whatever. A good boat for a carp angler should measure about 6ft (1.8m) lengthways inside and about 4ft (1.3m) across the width. Depending on the sort of fishing you are going to be doing, one of this size should be sufficient for one person and enough tackle for a few days.

The two models I use are both made by Zodiac. The gear boat goes under the name of Sevylor Fish Hunter and is marketed as a four-man boat. I chose this boat mainly because of its size but also because it has four inflatable chambers, which makes it ideal for carrying enough gear for one person for a week. One chamber is never enough, and neither are two when you consider the amount of gear we each use. I much prefer a boat that has several chambers. Apart from anything else, you never know when one chamber might let you down, and this is an especially important consideration if you have some distance to travel back to the car and safety.

My main boat is a Zodiac S131 four-man boat, which, like my gear one, has four different chambers. It has a collapsible wooden floor, which folds into three sections of 3 × 4ft (90 × 120cm). It is quite a big boat, and to be honest I could use both this and my gear boat for transporting two anglers and their gear for two weeks of fishing easily. Whether I do or not though is all dependent on the weather and the type of water I'm targeting. I don't like packing any boat full for long journeys, even less so in very windy conditions. No matter how stable a boat looks or feels in the margins, when you are out in the middle of it things are quite different. Some of the winds in places like Chantecoq are horrendous, and it is always better to think safety first.

ESSENTIAL BOAT EQUIPMENT

Before you even start to think about placing yourself and your gear into your boat or boats, you should always ensure that you have a few essential items on board. A good pair of oars and rowlocks are an absolute must, even if you are taking a motor along with you. I much prefer the wooden ones to the metal type as I find them stronger. I also prefer the type of rowlocks that enclose the oar and lock it into place. It's such a pain trying to row against a strong wind if the oars keep popping out. They should also be equipped with stoppers so that they are fixed into the rowlocks and not able to slide through. You will also need a torch, some flares, a life jacket, an anchor of some sort, a tow rope, a pump (if you are using an inflatable), a repair kit (quick-drying fibreglass for permanent boats or a puncture kit for the inflatables) as well as a spare battery and some spare sheer pins for the motor. I like to keep all of this stuff in a little plastic box that is watertight. A waterproof torch is also advisable.

I know some of you might laugh at the suggestion that you put flares in a carp boat, but what would you do if you were out in the middle of Chantecoq (over 10,000 acres) all by yourself and a problem occurred? The nearest angler isn't always going to be ten yards away from your bivvy, as in England. He is more likely to be half a mile away. The point is, you just never know. There have been too many boat disasters at carp fisheries over the last fifteen years. It is always better to be safe than sorry.

The Minn Kota engines are the most popular. Choose one with variable speed settings, both forward and reverse.

If you value your life, obviously it goes without saying that you should wear a life jacket at all times. If you don't, well, that's up to you, but you'd be a fool to go anywhere on water without one. I use the Fox KS version, which is the best I know. It is lightweight, green in colour and folds away to a tiny little size. I know that CEMEX Angling also sell an excellent jacket, as do many of the top tackle shops, but I challenge anyone who doesn't like the Fox KS.

Although you can use petrol motors on some waters around the world, most of the time you are limited to using a battery-operated one. This is the case in France, where you need to have a licence to use a petrol motor. The biggest name on the market for battery motors is Minn Kota. They offer a wide range of models, each with different speed settings and gadgets. I use an Endura 55, which has five different forward speeds and three back. It has 55lb

(25kg) of thrust and will pull my two boats very easily, even against the strongest of winds. A minimum of four different forward speeds and a reverse is absolutely necessary for all types of boat work. You need to conserve energy in the battery as much as you can, especially if you are planning on a few days away, which is one reason why I recommend the different speeds. I prefer to row as much as possible and use the motor for the times when the wind picks up and it gets difficult. I also use it for boating baits out and playing fish if I am by myself, and the variable speed settings will help you no end there.

The engine will be powered by a leisure battery, preferably the high-phase type which releases the power much more gradually than car batteries do. I always carry two of these in the boat. One is used as my reserve, the other for main usage. These you can get from any camping and caravan shop. At full charge, two will last me about two weeks for a trip to somewhere like Chantecoq. If you intend staying somewhere for longer than this, a good tip is to buy a solar charger for them. Although this will not charge a battery up from flat, it will trickle charge one and keep a relatively full one almost topped up.

USING THE BOAT

Boats are not just useful for moving from swim to swim, transporting gear, playing fish or baiting up. They also come in very handy for searching out the carp and any potential feeding areas. Ask any of the lads who fish Wraysbury what the most valuable piece of equipment is aside from the rods, reels, etc. Almost all of them will say a boat. Why? Basically because Wraysbury is full of all sorts of nooks and crannies and islands where the carp can hide away. You would never see the fish from the bank in

When the weather changes quickly, you can see exactly why you need a life jacket!

many of their favourite haunts, and the same goes for other big waters, too.

Using a boat to search out the carp though is an art. It isn't a case of just getting in and off you go. Far from it. You need to keep your eyes open and you need to be stealthy. The carp can see very easily directly above the water, which is why we are all advised to keep low to the ground when looking in on them. If you are standing up in a boat, there is a good chance they will see you as you get close to them, and that is assuming you haven't already spooked them with the sound of the engine or the splashing of the oars.

A couple of other pieces of kit that I could have included in the previous section

but have saved for here are polarizing glasses and a plastic goldfish tank. Polarizing glasses come in very handy for taking the glare off the water surface, but even these won't help you when there is a good chop present. This is where the fish tank comes in. I use one of the types that has a square flat bottom. It is made from plastic and very lightweight. When it's windy, you sit at the back of the boat and place the tank over the side, taking care not to fill it with water; you will find you are able to look beneath the ripple and glare very easily. It's of no use on murky water or deep venues, but where it is crystal clear or relatively shallow, it is excellent for looking for clear areas, fish, or whatever. A good tip, especially on

Wraysbury, a place where you'd never find the fish without a boat.

sunny days, is to keep the sun behind you, and cast a shadow with the boat on the water. This will take even more of the glare off the water and will aid your visibility somewhat. Some of my mates prefer to use goggles or face masks instead of tanks because they say that they can get a closer look. The choice is yours.

Another piece of kit that I should include here is an echo-sounder. On the big continental waters they really are essential because trying to use a plumbing rod at a place like Cassien or Chantecoq would be a complete waste of time. I use an Eagle Portable Fish ID, which is a really basic model. You don't need the sort that the deep-sea trawlers use, so don't be influenced into spending silly money

when all you need is something that will give you a simple understanding of what is underneath the boat. I use my sounder mainly for feature finding rather than for fish finding – to help me find clear areas amongst weed or to identify the depth of water, any silty areas or hard patches. All of the basic sounders have what is known as a grey line facility which enables you to see what the lake bed is like. This will show a grey line at the bottom of the screen: the thinner the line, the softer the bottom. For really hard patches of gravel or rock the line will be thicker.

As a back-up to the sounder, I carry a spare rod loaded with a heavy lead at all times. I use this to 'donk' the lead on the bottom to investigate any areas I want to know more about. Usually I load this with a spool of braid since this gives you a better 'feel' of any vibrations sent down the line. Any areas that take my fancy I then drop a marker on, usually the H-block type (available through Gardner Tackle) or a simple ballcock loaded with line and a lead.

An alternative way of marking a nice-looking feature or spot is to use a GPS system. Obviously you will need the right map to be able to do this if you are in a foreign country, but even at home such systems can be of great benefit. Although some GPS systems are not accurate down to the exact inch, they are ideal for marking sunken snags or areas where you have had pick-ups. They also come in useful for plotting swims just in case you have to

Echo-sounders are essential items of kit for the big waters, with the grey line facility coming in really handy.

A look at some of the essential items of gear needed in the boat, in this case with the echo-sounder screwed into place.

launch at night and aren't exactly sure where you are supposed to be heading.

THE PLAYING GAME

Playing fish from a boat is a real art, especially if you are on your own. Some of the very best I have seen doing it include Steve Briggs, Paul Hunt of Rainbow Carp Tours, and Rene Hawkins. If you are teamed up with a novice angler then I suggest going out by yourself rather than with the other angler at the engine. If he has no experience of rowing or steering, you may end up in all sorts of situations you don't really want to be, such as the boat going round in circles or offline because the oarsman has no sense of direction. Teamwork is the key to doing this with another, with the boat man being the main person in charge.

On your own, you will need an engine to help you. There is no use even attempting to try to land a fish without any power behind you. All that will happen is the fish will pull you all over the place, and if it's quite windy you may have extra problems to deal with because the boat will be blown off course. I speak from experience here. The boat may go in one direction while the fish goes in another. Trying to draw a fish over a net while the boat is getting blown along is impossible; you're pulling, but the boat is going backwards so you don't make up any distance. Not only that, even if it is flat calm, as soon as you try to put any side strain on a fish the boat will just go around in circles because it isn't fixed into position. This is a nightmare situation, and one that can be countered only by a source of power pushing in the opposite direction.

The ideal when playing from a boat is always to keep the fish well away from you. Imagine that the boat is the land. Try to maintain at least a rod's length of dis-

tance between you and where the fish is. If it swims towards you, then slam the engine in reverse. If it goes away from you, then whack it into forward thrust. If it goes to the side, make ground on it by steering in the relevant direction. The only time you want to get any closer to that fish is when it is ready for netting. Even then, though, placing the net in the water presents its own difficulties because as you push the net forwards the boat will go backwards! The only way to do it is to lower the net below the water and draw the fish towards you. A short net-pole such as the Hutchinson two-piece Carp Q will help here. Use this on the shorter section only and you won't have any options other than to sink it and draw the fish to it – it's too short to do anything else. Draw the fish slowly to the net, adjusting the power on the engine whenever necessary. It's a balancing act really, with the angler needing all of his motor skills to make a good job of it, keeping one hand as close to the engine as possible just in case some extra thrust is needed.

As with everything, the first few times you play any fish in a boat, you will run into problems no doubt. Just keep a tight line on it and keep it well away from the engine prop! Practice makes perfect, as they say.

PUTTING THE BAITS OUT

On the really big waters where you need to fish further out than you can cast, you will need to boat your baits out – something that can be done in two ways. You can either leave the rod on the bank and take the hookbait only out with you, or you can take the rod as well. I've tried both methods, but Steve Briggs persuaded me that taking the rod as well is by far the best way, and he was right.

It is a lot easier to keep a straight line when you have the rod in your hands than it is if you don't, especially if there is a strong chop on the water and you are by yourself. If you take the lead only, you end up with line all over the place, and if you go off course there is the chance that it may get caught up around a bale arm, buzzer head or indicator on the bank, making for completely wasted effort. If it does become tangled around something it will put tension on the line, which will cause the rig to go shooting out of the boat and get stuck in an obstruction (possibly your leg or hand!).

I needed to go out in the boat on my own to land this mid-thirty Cassien mirror, freeing it from several weed beds in 30ft (90m) of water.

An ocean of water and a lone angler makes his way back to land after placing his baits out. There is no way of fishing such a big lake other than with a boat.

Another plus-point about taking the rod with you is that you will have more time to examine the lake bed and identify exactly where you want to drop your rig. When done, all you then need to do is head to shore and tighten things up.

6 The Business End

What good would a book on carp fishing be without some chit-chat about rigs? Everyone loves to look at gadgets and talk about what works or doesn't on the lakes that we fish. Instead of going over old ground and talking about the basics, though, I wish to present discussion, which will hopefully stimulate thought.

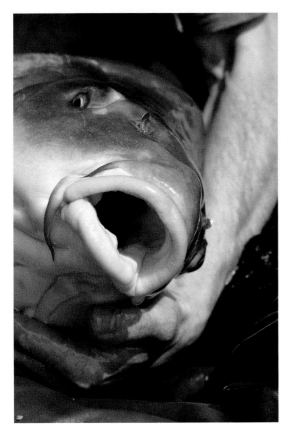

Catch me if you can!

How better to begin than with an interview with the rig guru himself, Frank Warwick. There's no one more qualified to talk about advanced carp rigs than Frank. He is the master of the mechanics. The following transcript was part of a series of articles for *Crafty Carper* magazine, and even to someone as rig simple as myself it is nothing if not thought-provoking.

If ever you have wanted to know how deeply some anglers think about this subject, then take this lot in. It's advanced carp fishing at its very highest level …

ADVANCED CARP FISHING RIGS
An Interview with Frank Warwick

Simon I don't know how many people take a look at the weekly magazine *Carp-Talk*, but a recent issue that caught my eye featured an article by Ken Townley talking about the palm test and its relevance to testing the efficiency of a rig. What are your thoughts on this one, mate?

Frank I saw the issue that you mention. Apart from getting cameras under water, as Danny Fairbrass and John Bannister have done in the Korda videos, a lot of us guess at what is actually occurring at the business end. I base everything that I do on comparisons in actual fishing circumstances. You need tangible proof basically. When I've tied up a rig on the bank, I see no problem with testing its efficiency by

The palm test gives Frank confidence that the mechanics of the rig (the flipping of the hook) are presenting the hook swiftly to the floor of the carp's mouth.

dragging it across the palm of my hand. I know it isn't a foolproof way of testing one, but it's a lot of hassle carrying around a mummified carp's head in my rucksack every time I go fishing!

Simon For the people that haven't read the piece, can you explain what Ken's angle was on this?

Frank First and foremost, I'll say that Ken is a friend of mine, and the article was very thought-provoking. He surmised that a palm in no way represents the make-up of a carp's mouth. He showed a rubber O ring that was about 2 inches across, which he used to represent a carp's lips. Correct me if I am wrong, but a rubber O ring isn't exactly foolproof either is it? Of course everything works differently under water so, with

this, the readers obviously have their first task – go and see for themselves. I'm not arrogant enough to say that the rig I use is better than Ken's, but at least with a palm test it clearly gives the angler confidence that the mechanics of the rig – the flipping of the hook – are presenting the hook swiftly to the floor of the carp's mouth.

Simon I see where Ken is coming from, for what my opinion is worth, but I must say that I agree with your O ring statement wholeheartedly. If you are going to knock the palm test, then at least give a better example than an O ring. I have caught countless carp in my time and dissected several, too, but never have I come across a ridge in the bottom of a carp's mouth that would be as pronounced as an O ring.

Frank Neither have I, which is why I have mentioned it. The rig I use has been tested on countless venues around the world, and I have total confidence in it. I know that if you use a proper line-aligner, you will have more converted takes than you would with say a simple knotless knot set-up [*see* Crowood's book *Strategic Carp Fishing* for bench test results]. For me, when I have fished one against the other, the line-aligner version has generally out-fished the other over a period of time. This isn't on one water either, but on several waters. I'm not naïve enough to think that this is the 'be all and end all' of everything because obviously it isn't.

Simon I'll make the point here that having fished a lot with you over the last few years, I have seen your rig result in more pick-ups than say a standard line-aligner rig. I have noticed you receive pick-ups at times when most others are not receiving any action whatsoever. I will say that you do lose a few along the way through hook pulls, perhaps because your rig turns silent periods into

Frank with a stunning common from tough day-ticket venue Hardwick Lake on the Linear Fisheries complex in Oxfordshire.

chances that might otherwise go unnoticed. Would you agree with this?

Frank Yes. We've both seen it.

Simon Let's talk about the palm test then. What are you looking for with it?

Frank Basically, I don't want my rig to lie so that the hook is sat on its side. It's a bit like a cat's claw skidding across your palm but not sticking in. I want mine to stick in instantly – whether this is caused by the fish tightening the hooklink or not, it doesn't matter. I just want the hook sat on its point, primed and ready to grip. Ken appears to be working on the principle that the carp will successfully turn the bait and the hook before ejecting it, which I under- stand. But with my rig, I am working on the basis that the hook lodges instantly in the flesh of the mouth and the fish then having difficulty ejecting it. A palm test, as I said before, shows me that once the rig is

95

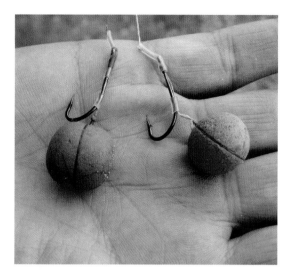

Close-up of the business end of Frank's rig –
a set-up that he believes results in more
pick-ups than a standard line-aligner rig.

One of Frank's little inventions: the shot on
the hook set-up.

The finger test. Frank's opinion is that
there is hardly any situation representative
of what a carp's mouth would be doing.

in the mouth, the hook has a very good
chance of turning and lodging a hold.

Simon   How often do you use the shot on
the hook rig to assist here, something that
you invented a few years back now?

Frank   I still use it quite a lot, but I have
found that the rig set-up I use today probably turns just as much without the shot
on as it would with it. The shot does, however, help the hook to get a hold inside the
mouth when the fish is sucking and blowing and trying to rid the rig.

Simon   What about the finger test? In
Ken's piece he mentioned that this would
be a more suitable test for checking a rig's
potential? Any comments on this?

Frank   A finger test is in my mind much
less realistic than any kind of test you can
try on the bank. It involves pulling a hooklink over a finger with the link at a right
angle to the bait. To me, there is hardly any
situation representative of what a carp's

mouth would be doing with this test. Certainly on some of the hard-fished UK waters where the carp are very wily, they are mouthing the hookbait only. They don't even suck it back into the mouth, they merely extend the protrusion of the mouth and sample it without moving their head out of position. This is where the palm test has relevance. Try it with my rig, and it will flip the hook almost instantly. When the fish realizes it is pricked, any head movement by it will, especially when using a sharp hook like I do, result in a pricking of the hook.

Simon What sort of hooks do you use?

Frank Long Shank Incizors most of the time. They are ultra sharp. I check the point every time I reel in or cast out, just to make sure mine have no burrs on them. If one does, I'll change it instantly. I'm a big believer that pricking the fish is the start of the chain reaction to actually hooking one confidently.

Simon After pricking one, are you relying on the length of the hooklink or the type of the hooklink to take over?

Frank Both really. If it's in the carp's mouth, it would be nice to get some indication to tell us this, but it isn't always possible with wily fish. The length and type of the hooklink are very important components of the rig. With some fish, even with the sharpest hooks in the world, they are so cute they will easily blow the best rig in the world out. Pricking them is the 'hoped for' start of the chain reaction of events. Using a stiff link in this situation would be the ideal because a carp would have difficulty blowing this out of the mouth, especially in the scenario that Ken was describing in his feature – where the rig would do a U-turn in the carp's mouth. On the other hand,

you may be faced with the problem of the rig not going in the mouth when using a stiff rig because its stiffness doesn't lend itself well to getting in the mouth, which is why Terry Hearn devised the stiff rig pop-up, or hinged stiff rig as some call it. It can stop the bait from behaving naturally. The obvious compromise is therefore to use a combi-rig, which is what I favour.

Simon How do you present this?

Frank It's quite straightforward really. I will use a prototype skinned link that I've been using for about five years now. I will peel back about an inch or two of the link closest to the hook, giving me the supple movement in that area. If I use pop-ups, I will present the shot/putty just up from the edge where the supple part meets the stiff section. I will always use a line-aligner, and I will form this by using some shrink tube pushed over the hook and steamed into position.

Simon One thing I hear a lot of talk on the bank about is the prototype hooklink that you use. Can you explain its properties to us?

Frank There are a few links out there on the market that have similar qualities, notably Armaled's Kik-Bac and Korda's Hybrid coated hooklink. It is a braided hooklink that is coated in a stiff plastic outer, which in Korda's case is fluorocarbon. It enables you to present a very stiff hooklink where you can make the last inch or less flexible to impart more natural movement to your hookbait, which in turn also allows the hook to twist and flip in the carp's mouth. Basically, you are getting the best of both worlds.

Simon Do you steam the link to straighten it or not?

Frank Yes, every time, over the top of a boiling kettle with the top open, pulling at each end to keep it straight. This helps to keep the hooklink flush to the bottom and, as a bonus, it always kicks the hookbait away from the lead. As soon as they take the rig into their mouth, they are instantly tensioning it up.

Simon All interesting and heavy stuff, but none of it is relevant if you can't get the carp picking up the bait in the first place. Would you agree?

Frank I agree. That's why using a good bait is just as important. I've said this many times before: it's a percentages thing.

In action at Orchid Lakes. Another one nears the net for Mr Warwick.

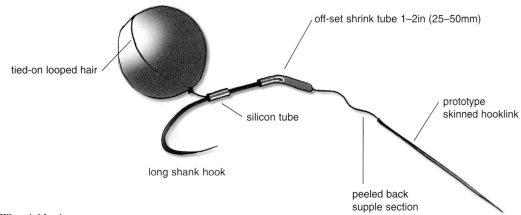

tied-on looped hair

off-set shrink tube 1–2in (25–50mm)

silicon tube

long shank hook

prototype
skinned hooklink

peeled back
supple section

Frank Warwick's rig.

Let's paint a scenario. Say, you choose a bait like peanuts at random and the fish are going berserk on them. You may have a very basic uncomplicated rig on there. Because the fish are so heavily on the nuts, it would appear that your rig doesn't matter. Because of repeated pick-ups, sooner or later, by sheer weight of odds, you would get a take on a basic rig. More fish will have had the rig in their mouth so the odds are you will eventually receive a pick-up. Take the good bait away, and you are dramatically reducing your odds, which brings us back to the efficiency of the rig. Quite often, a good application of a bait will make a basic rig look useful, but if you turn it on its head, just how good would a very good bait be with a very good rig? There would be no contest would there? The old adage 'keep it simple' doesn't wash with me. The rig I use has been described as clinical rather than simple, and I tend to agree with that. Tim Paisley, as an example, used to rely on bait application and the quality of it, but as soon as he gravitated to what many would describe as a more sophisticated rig, his catch rate visibly improved, something that he himself has acknowledged in print before now.

Perfect!

99

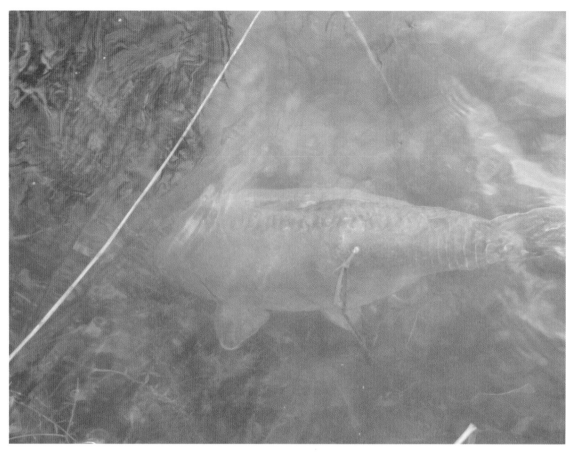

Quite often, a good application of a bait will make a basic rig look useful, but just how good would a very good bait be with a very good rig? Food for thought.

If we had a little counter every time a fish mouthed our rigs, I think we would all be greatly surprised. You only have to look at fish when they feed on the surface to see that carp can easily select out the freebait [from the one] with the hook in it. Something just isn't quite right for them, which is why they leave them until last. Catching carp successfully is like a big jig-saw, where each piece has to go into a certain place. There is nothing wrong with using the palm test as a guide to the efficiency of a rig. I use it all the time and I will continue using it for many years to come, or until someone comes up with a better way of testing a rig on the bank, which, to date, no one has done.

Simon Thanks mate. We'll end it there. Brilliant stuff.

TRANSCRIPT SUMMARY

Frank's thinking behind rigs is amazing and I'm sure the transcript has given you much to think about. Having known him for many years now and spent many a long, dark night chatting away with him in the bivvy, you can't not learn something from him. He has watched carp close up feeding on bait countless times, and has caught some of the toughest fish in the country.

I particularly found the part where he talks about the palm test the most interesting. I have used it for many years – since I read an article by Rob Maylin who was advocating it. It is impossible to check the exact turning capabilities of a rig when inside a carp's mouth because water plays such an important part. In the underwater carping DVDs by Korda, which came out in 2004, it was clear to see that water helps the carp rid itself of even the most sophisticated of rigs easily. No rig is ever going to be 100 per cent foolproof, but having one that flips the hook gives the angler so much confidence that testing it for this property can only be beneficial.

Frank's rig is widely regarded as being the best hooker in the business. It pricks carp when other rigs don't seem to get them, but having seen him use it, and having tried it myself, I must say that it does lose a few fish along the way, which is something that I myself have trouble getting my

Another one bites the dust! Frank with another fine fish from Hardwick Lake.

head around. I much prefer to have a higher ratio of hooked and landed fish, since I'm convinced that carp communicate with one another. A lost fish has consequences, not only from the results perspective: I firmly believe it leads to the end of any future action, whereas a landed fish often sees more fish come your way.

By not using Frank's advocated rig, I suppose I'm being ignorant because there are thousands of anglers out there who use it successfully. However, I hope you'll see throughout this chapter, and indeed the book, that successful carp fishing is also about being confident. The topic of rigs is a personal thing that is driven by self-belief. I have rigs that work for me – rigs that have caught me fish from the easiest of the easiest lakes to the hardest of the hard, and for many, many years.

I'm not going to even try to convince you that my rigs are the only way forwards because they quite obviously are not. This chapter is aimed at provoking thought. I want to get you thinking about strategy, a horrible word that governs a lot of success in carp fishing. Heavy stuff I know, but many experienced anglers will tell you that you are not going to get better by choosing a rig because it looks good or because it caught Joe Bloggs twenty different forties in a week. You need to know how something works, and when something should be used. The only way I can get this message across is by taking a look at some of my own thoughts on why and when I use the rigs that I do.

MY RIGS

Uni-Rig

In the past I've written a lot about a rig called the Uni-Rig, indicating that this takes up approximately 75 per cent of my fishing. I've not written about much else when it comes to this topic, but if I said I didn't use anything else I'd be lying, which is why I want to delve into my thinking behind it now.

Over the years I have seen some superb articles and talks about rigs. Probably one of the best talks I've ever seen, one that I was enthralled by, was given by carp tackle manufacturer Kevin Nash in Sheffield. At the time, Kev opened my eyes to the world of 'heavy thinking' and how I'd be a fool to dismiss rigs as just rigs. He also made me aware that I should be 'working off' one rig rather than using just one rig in my armoury. It was around this time that I was fishing a lot of day-ticket waters on a one-off basis for monthly reviews in *Carpworld* magazine. Most of my rig writing then was based on the Uni-Rig, which is as basic as a rig can come (a standard braided hooklink, usually 25lb Super Nova of between 8 and 12in, knotless knotted to the chosen hook and then line-aligned). Regardless of its name, I don't for one minute think it is a universal carp rig that will outcatch all other rigs, end of story. It was given the name principally because it is as universal as a carp rig can get, and proved especially effective for me and Rob Hughes when fishing blind (not knowing much about a water) on the English day-ticket circuit. It served its purpose exceptionally well, and I still believe that you won't come across a better way of approaching the unknown.

Having caught carp from upwards of 200 different waters though, I know full well that the Uni-Rig isn't the be-all and end-all of carp rigs. It is the rig I work off and have total confidence in for 75 per cent of the situations I encounter. For the other 25 per cent I need to have alternatives. Being a simple rig fan, I'd love to believe that I can conquer the world with only one rig, but I really would be kidding myself. There are just too many carp in this world for them all to be identical. Like it or

The Uni-Rig.

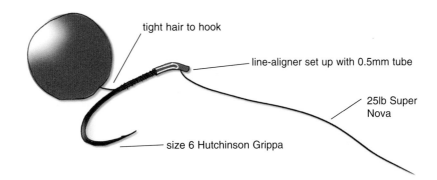

tight hair to hook

line-aligner set up with 0.5mm tube

25lb Super Nova

size 6 Hutchinson Grippa

lump it, even someone as rig-blinkered as I needs to have alternatives, which is why I have variations of both the stiff and combination rigs in my armoury.

Stiff Rig

I don't think I need to talk in-depth about the type of stiff rig I use as it is dead basic: 20lb monofilament or bigger, or Amnesia in the 30lb size. I've also used a selection of the flourocarbons a few times, including Suffix's Invisiline and Carp 'R' Us Ghoul.

Much of the reason why people use stiff rigs is the anti-ejection properties of them. I acknowledge this sort of thinking, but these days – about ten years on from when the first writings about stiff rigs hit the press – I'm sure a lot of carp are now wise to them, especially the very pressured ones in the circuit waters. Instead I tend to believe that stiff rigs are a way of giving the angler confidence because they rarely tangle and also because they are a lot more durable.

Monolines are a heck of a lot tougher than braids. Do the tests and see for yourself. Some monos, I will admit, are not very strong, but if you select a tough version, such as Nash Bullet, Berkley Big Game or Fox Soft Steel, you'll see what I'm getting at. These lines are so much tougher than standard braided hooklinks, such as Super Nova, Silkworm or any

other top brand, that they are the only real choice for tough fishing amongst snags.

I've lost so many fish over the years by thinking that I can get away with braid that mono stiff rigs are now my only choice for these situations. I've even tried keeping the braid to a small, less obtrusive length so that it has very little chance of touching sharp objects, but even 6in (15cm) lengths are prone to cutting when fished in difficult surroundings. Braids cut too easily for my liking, which is why I opt for the monos for overseas waters like Raduta, Cassien or similar. I know a lot of you reading this may not be interested in fishing these waters but, take it from me, even on your local day-ticket water there will be times when braided hooklinks won't be up to the job. A couple of years ago, I lost a decent fish on Withy Pool because the hooklink touched the branches of a tree. On that water, I had not lost any fish in those circumstances before, so don't dismiss its happening at your water. I'm a massive fan of braids, but you just can't get away with using them for all situations.

Stiff Rig Pop-Up Rig

I have never dismissed any ideas, but when it comes to rigs I've tended to shy away from bits and pieces that look complicated. I must admit that I first looked at this pop-

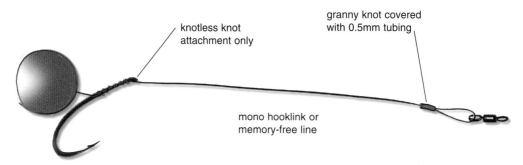

knotless knot
attachment only

granny knot covered
with 0.5mm tubing

mono hooklink or
memory-free line

The stiff rig.

up rig in this way, which was down to igno-rance more than anything else.

Fishing a pop-up on a standard stiff rig leaves the pop-up only a short distance off the lake bed, even if you set it at 10in (25cm) on a 20in (50cm) link. The reason this happens is that the link has no pivot, so it just bends upwards, which causes resistance on the hookbait, pulling it clos-er to the lake bed. The stiff rig pop-up rig has it dead right. It allows the hook to be positioned at the right distance 90 degrees to the hooklink, which really is where we want it.

The way I set it up is simple. I just insert a Solar Ball Bearing Flexi-Ring swivel to the hooklink at the distance where I want the bait to pop up. I then add some putty,

Stiff rig pop-up. Use mono or Amnesia line. Attach the hook to the line with a knotless knot. Loop the ends through the swivels, and then tie securely with a granny knot. Cover the knots with 0.5mm silicon tube.

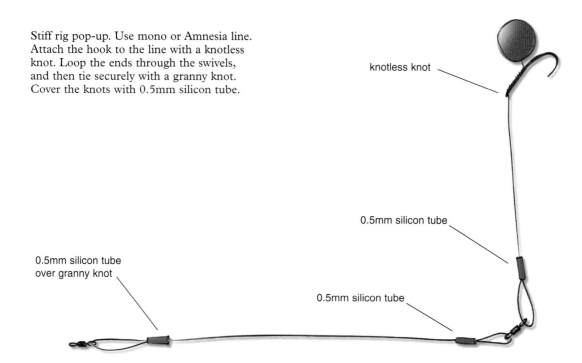

knotless knot

0.5mm silicon tube

0.5mm silicon tube
over granny knot

0.5mm silicon tube

if required, to where the swivel is located. I always keep at least one eye of the swivel free from the putty, just to stop any tangles or problems from occurring.

The components of this rig are usually a size 4 or 6 Hutchinson Precision hook, the hooklink in two different strengths; the top half is of a lighter strength than the main section (usually I opt for a 35lb strength for the main length, with the hook attachment being of 20lb). The ring swivel I use is a size 8. I think the smaller the swivel the better here. I could use a bigger one, thus adding more weight to the pop-up, meaning less putty, but I don't like bulky swivels. This is because I've had tangle problems with big bulky swivels, even with strong hooklinks. I don't like much putty either, preferring Kryson's Heavy Metal Plus, which is a superb product when you don't like much putty on the rig. The only other component worth commenting on is the addition of some 0.5mm tubing. I add an inch of this to cover the overhand knots in the rig – basically to prevent tangles and to make the whole thing look neat and tidy.

A well-framed Cassien mirror that fell foul of the stiff rig pop-up.

The business end of a stiff rig pop-up.

Combi-Rig

I use the comb-rig for the pressured venues, mainly because a lot of my mates have faith in it. So many anglers over the last couple of years have been catching well on this rig that I just couldn't ignore it. Steve Briggs, Tim Paisley, Frank Warwick, plus several other friends, have been using variations of it to overcome bait-ejection problems encountered on some tricky English

venues. Birch Grove is one such water where I've tried it and caught. I was getting aborted takes, a single bleep followed by a slight drop back, and a strike into nothing, but a change to this rig soon sorted it.

I use only one type of combi-rig, and this is probably the most widely known and used in the industry at the present moment. Using either Kryston's Mantis Gold, Snake-Skin or Armaled's Kik-Bac I peel back the end nearest the hook and then attach it to this via a knotless knot (so that I have a supple hair as well), ensuring that approximately an inch up from the hook is supple. I like the supple section to be no more than an inch as I am trying to offer the carp no margin for error. Any more than this I'm sure that the rig is wasted as a combination link, and I may as well offer the whole rig as a supple braid. To complete the rig, I use the line-aligner slipped over the eye of the hook and attach the whole thing to a swivel in the same way that I do all stiff rigs (via a simple looped knot, which is then protected by a small piece of 0.5mm tubing). I like to think that the carp may be able to blow this rig around its mouth, but it

The combi-rig.

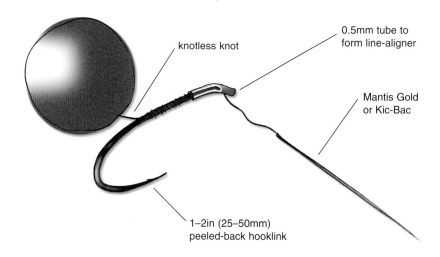

knotless knot

0.5mm tube to
form line-aligner

Mantis Gold
or Kic-Bac

1–2in (25–50mm)
peeled-back hooklink

Rob Hughes with a Horseshoe Lake mirror caught using a combi-rig presentation.

For bottom-bait presentations, I favour the hair coming off the side of the hook.

won't be able to blow it out (the stiff part prevents this).

Although this type of set-up is not exactly new to the carp fishing arena, I think that it is at least newer/fresher than other presentations. If I come across what I believe are wily, rig-shy carp, I bring this out of the wallet, using it for about 5 to 10 per cent of my fishing at the moment.

Hair Attachment

With most of my rigs, even the Uni-Rig, I tie the hair off the side of the hook because I believe it may help the rig to twist in the mouth of the carp, and thus enhance the hooking capabilities of the rig. I have never carried out any scientific tests on this (as Rob Hughes and I did with the line-aligner, knotless knot, and so on, in *Strategic Carp Fishing*), so I cannot confirm my beliefs. Basically, I use it because I think it will do no harm to the set-up whilst at the same time possibly increasing my chances.

When the hair comes off the back of the hook, the weight of a bottom bait will leave the hook lying point upwards when in the mouth of the carp, especially with the tight hair presentation I favour. If the carp sits ever so still, it will therefore be able to eject it successfully. Off the side, it will leave the hook lying on its side, with the point closer to the flesh of the mouth.

The only time I won't attach the hair to the side of the shank is when using pop-ups. For this type of presentation, I favour the hair coming off the back of the hook, almost exactly opposite the point. This is simply so that the hook sits proud, right underneath the bait, and is not set to the side, which could, in essence, lead to a poor hook hold when the bait is being approached off the bottom.

Lead or Stonze?

I am not going to dwell on the topic of leads in this book because we covered them extensively in *Discover Carp Fishing*. The type I use has not changed at all in the six years since we wrote that book and, apart from some fancy packaging and well-designed marketing, neither has the market place.

One question I hear many anglers asking though is whether or not there is a need to move off leads and onto the Stonze, which are being sold by Pallatrax. The use of stones on the end of a line goes back years and well before Jens Bursell wrote an informative *Carpworld* article about fishing at Lake Raduta in 1998: he tied rocks to the end of his lines to keep his baits in the water when the wind started to blow at the infamous world-record venue. In fact, before we were all lads, anglers used to tie stones on the end of the line as a weight, and at Pallatrax they have basically picked up on this very simple idea and taken it further. Can't blame 'em really can you? What an easy way to make money – drill a hole in the end of a stone, fix a swivel within it, and hey presto you have a money-maker that will give a lot of anglers confidence, which at the end of the day is what it's all about.

I don't think the lead is about to bow out just yet though. They are just too convenient. They cast so very easily and they allow us to hook carp very easily because their size-to-weight ratio is perfect for the angling situation (the Stonze aren't as aerodynamic or as heavy). As for the comments I hear about carp wising up to leads on the bottom and stones being more natural, well I really can't grasp that. If a lead has blown then surely there must be too many of them in the lake. And if that is the case then surely they are as natural to the carp as a stone. In any case, if there are so many natural-looking stones on the bottom then what's to stop your lead coming to rest against one of these? This is where this whole argument stops in my book

The Stonze, a simple yet ingenious invention.

because you just can't convince me that a carp can tell the difference between a stone and a lead just by looking at it – there has to be more to it.

Although it sounds like I have just slated the Stonze and tried to convince everyone not to fall for the hype, I'm actually of the opinion that they definitely have an advantage over the lead in one particular area, which is why I will always carry a few around in my tackle box. Let me explain.

Sorry to get into a deep conversation here, but does anyone remember the articles by Mike Wilson, which appeared in *Carp Fisher* in the mid-1980s or thereabouts? Perhaps some of the older anglers will. If I remember rightly, Mike wrote about the tiny electrical charge that a lead can emit when it is submerged in water. At the time of writing I think Mike was fishing Savay, and he referred to the charge given off when two different metals come into contact with one another, which he believed fish disliked, assisting the carp to single out the hookbait. The reaction he

109

Carp have very refined receptors, which can sense all sorts of vibrations in water very easily.

referred to was caused by the lead and the swivel section coming into contact with one another.

We should all know that carp have very refined receptors, which will sense all sorts of reactions or vibrations in water very easily. They can sense even the tiniest of vibrations via their lateral line system as well as in the ears (which combined make up the acoustic-lateralis system), and they can also receive signals via their other lesser receptors, which are located all over the body. It is these senses that allow them to detect anglers when they so much as place a foot on the bank of a lake.

Some anglers talk freely about carp sensing vibrations sent via echo-sounders and such things so it certainly doesn't seem so improbable that they can sense even the slightest electrical energy from a lead does it? I know it might sound like taking things a bit too far – because carp are after all a very simple creature since they get caught even on leads – but if the fishing is hard and you really do have to scratch around for a bite then there might just be something in this reaction thing. Let's take a further look at what Mike wrote to explain this.

To overcome the reaction created by the two metals coming into contact with one another, Mike suggested using glass chandelier pieces as weights. These would act as buffers. Using the glass weights presented all sorts of problems to him, however, such as restricted casting distance and coming off the rig once they hit the lake bed. But, if I remember rightly, when he tried the two methods against one another he found that when he presented the glass weight successfully there was, at certain times, a definite increase in his catch rate.

There are times when whatever you throw at the fish they will have it. There are other times when they can be a bit fussy, but you'll still catch 'em if you stick at it. But I think we all recognize there are other times when they get downright choosy. These are the moments when the thinking anglers begin to shine through; these are the periods when we need to do something out of the ordinary to get a bite. We have to out-think the fish, and this is perhaps when their guard is right up and they pick out even the slightest of danger signs easily.

I mentioned earlier that I can't ever see the lead being replaced by something else, but if the fishing is particularly tricky then you might be wise to turn your attentions to the Stonze. I've never done any tests, but I would imagine that they would be less likely to emit the charge that Mike believed a lead with a swivel does so; they might just give you the edge to unlocking a motionless indicator period. They aren't as practical as a lead, but so long as we take this into consideration they must still be worth a try.

RIGS OVERVIEW – GETTING IT RIGHT

One of my mates, Derek Fell, recently said that if you credit carp with a fair amount of intelligence you are on the right lines because you will try harder to outwit them

and will apply more thought to your fishing. In some respects, I tend to agree with what Derek says, but I also think that carp are not as intelligent as perhaps some anglers suggest. They are wild creatures, and they don't think as we do – even when educated by angling pressure. Carp are not capable of out-thinking anglers, that's a fact. The main thing they have to their advantage is that they can sense danger better than we do. That is how they survive.

Carp have a 'sixth sense' if you like, something that I touched on in Chapter 1. I don't like to call it a form of intelligence because I honestly believe that, if it was, there wouldn't be the times when they appear to be so easy to catch. We all know that even on the most pressured carp water, there is a period, be it only a few minutes or whatever, when the carp drop their guard. It happens so often and so seasonally that you can almost set your calendar by

The humble lead is not yet ready to die out.

it. Why would this happen if a carp was intelligent and could tell the difference between one rig bit and another? If someone can answer that for me then I'll perhaps change my view on the topic of rigs. However, I don't know anyone who can, which is why most of my fishing is based on what I consider to be a logical and fairly simple approach. I think if a carp senses danger it will identify the hookbait a lot easier than some people think, without even sampling it, even when using the most in-vogue presentations.

I can remember fishing at the infamous Lake Raduta in Romania in 2000. Derek Fell, who I was fishing with, was convinced I wasn't catching the bigger fish because of my rigs. I disagreed. The bigger fish, he thought, were harder to catch because they were wary of the rigs I was using (12in mono hooklinks knotless knotted to size 2 hooks). By the end of the trip, I was hauling stockies out like there was no tomorrow, but no signs of anything better than low-thirties. Two days in, Derek managed a nice 47lb and a low-thirty on the same rigs I was

A lovely 30lb common is displayed to the camera. Why is it that some carp single out and avoid hookbaits one minute, and then get caught the next?

using, which turned out to be the best fish between us. As the trip progressed and the fishing got tougher, he fiddled with his rigs (shortening, lengthening, scaling down, tubing here and there, and so on), changing this, changing that, but nothing better came along. Why? Well, for one, I think it was because there were so many stockies in the area we were fishing it was a matter of probability which size fish came along. We also fell short in the bait department, too. We opted for high-attract baits for the trip, which I think was a big mistake.

In my mind, rigs don't have as much influence on big carp as bait and location. In fact, I'd go as far as to say that rigs don't have as much influence on carp of any size as bait and location do. I don't believe there are rigs that are big carp pullers, even the ones that carp angling legend Terry Hearn uses. What many people forget is that Terry fishes waters that tend to contain a better than average size of carp than those that most of us fish. I'm not saying that's the main reason he catches lots of big fish. Far from it. I think Terry is just exceptionally gifted at working out how best to target waters. He is 'in tune' and capable of increasing his chances for lots of reasons – not just the rig he uses. He uses a bait that he knows carp like, and gets the positioning, baiting and location so very, very right.

I went through a stage a couple of years ago of messing around with my rigs, thinking that they were the reason that I wasn't being very successful with the bigger fish on some of the waters I was fishing. That year I sat out the winter syndicate at Birch Grove (November to March – and it was extended into April) for only two fish. During that time Jon 'Shoes' Jones landed eight. It was Jon's first winter on the water and I thought I had the place sussed until then. I stripped down Shoes's approach until I thought I'd found where my prob-

lem was. At first I thought it was my baiting strategies, but others convinced me it was my rig. I'd had a few little twitches during the winter, which had resulted in nothing. Shoes didn't have any of these so I thought it had to be down to my rigs, which is why I started messing. It carried on past the winter months, with my losing a few at Motorway Pond in the spring, and then at Tilery, and then at The Mangrove and a couple of overseas venues. Basically, I never got settled on the rigs I was using.

The following winter I was back where I started because I concluded it wasn't a rig

Come to daddy! Was the rig its downfall?

thing that had caused me to struggle so much at Birch (although that did inevitably lead to my problems later on in the year); it was instead my tactical approach. Shoes was using single hookbaits while I was focusing mainly on baited areas, a tactic I'd had a lot of success with at the venue in the past. I know baited areas pull carp in winter. I've had too many fish on them to think otherwise. However, what I'd done that year was to pay too much attention to that approach, almost to the point that I was disregarding all others.

Maybe I'm wrong in what I've written, maybe I'm right. It is just one of those things that I can only speculate about. I don't like confusing matters more than they need to be. I've done that far too many times in my fishing, and usually it has centred on my rigs. Nowadays I prefer to lean more towards being confident in what I am doing, and this is a subject that can best wrap up this topic: to finish this chapter I'm going to take a look at the favoured rigs used by three of the UK's most high-profile anglers – all different, and all concrete evidence that confidence is the key component to getting your head around this amazingly complex subject. There is no wonder-rig on the market, just lots of different items that need to be placed into a rig to make the angler confident in what he is doing. Confidence comes only with experience. It can't be bought over the counter or learnt through any book or magazine. It comes from time on the bank. I'll end this one there.

TOP RIGS BY TOP ANGLERS

Steve Briggs:

'For several years now I've relied heavily on combi-rigs of one form or another. The fact that they can be adjusted so easily to suit the situation, and they are also very effective, means that I've rarely needed to look any further. For fishing on home lakes or small, snag-free waters, the rig tends to be made from a stiff section of 25lb Amnesia leading up to a softer section of braid at the hook end, which is generally 25lb Super-Nova. For tougher situations I change the materials, and for really snaggy waters I normally go up to 50lb Berkley Fireline for the stiff section and 50lb Korda Arma-Kord for the remainder.

'The stiff section is always the longest part of the hook length at about 7in, while the softer section is between 1in and 3in. The two materials are joined via a small rig

Steve Briggs's favoured rig.

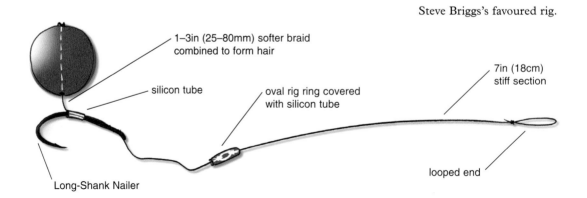

1–3in (25–80mm) softer braid combined to form hair

silicon tube

oval rig ring covered with silicon tube

7in (18cm) stiff section

looped end

Long-Shank Nailer

ring. The hooks used are mainly Long-Shank Nailers but I also use Hutchinson Precisions at times. The combi-rig serves several purposes: the stiff section always presents the hookbait well on the bottom and it is also fairly anti-tangle, but it is also a very effective hooking rig and the small amount of play that the fish have with the rig means they are less likely to be able to reject the rig successfully.'

International Carp Angler of the Year 2004 and 2005, Steve Briggs, with a 58lb Lake Raduta mirror.

The business end of Steve's favoured rig.

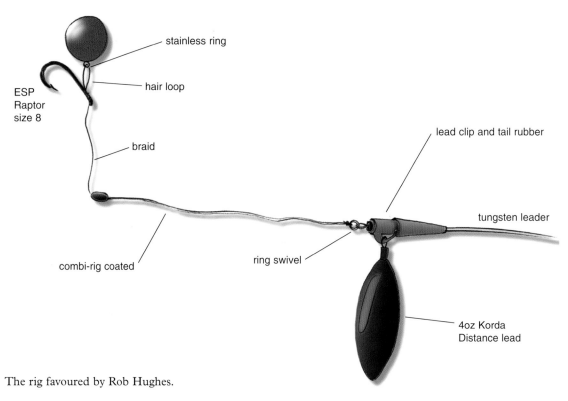

stainless ring

hair loop

ESP
Raptor
size 8

lead clip and tail rubber

braid

tungsten leader

combi-rig coated

ring swivel

4oz Korda
Distance lead

The rig favoured by Rob Hughes.

Rob Hughes:

'I don't feel that there is a rig that suits every eventuality, and as a result I have three rigs that I use for virtually all of my fishing. The only variation to them is the hook size and the length of the hair. They are: a supple rig, which is a 4–6in braided link shrink tube line-aligned to a size 8 hook; a stiff rig, which is a 10in flourocarbon hooklink looped at the swivel and tied knotless knot to the hook; and the last one

Rob with a 30lb-plus mirror from an undisclosed Berkshire stillwater.

is an 8in combi-rig that is a peelable braided hooklink with 1in peeled back, looped to the swivel and shrink tube line-aligned to a size 6 hook. The only other criteria is that the hooks must be absolutely pin sharp!'

A stunning summer-caught French mirror for Jon 'Shoes' Jones, proving that confidence in a good rig is the key to catching carp successfully.

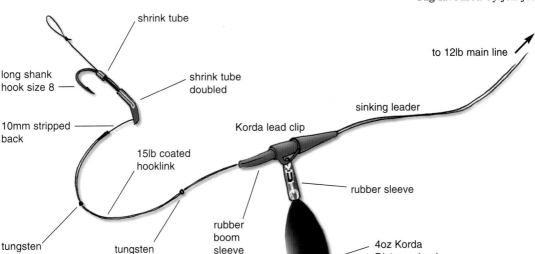

Rig favoured by Jon Jones.

shrink tube

long shank
hook size 8

shrink tube
doubled

to 12lb main line

10mm stripped
back

sinking leader

Korda lead clip

15lb coated
hooklink

rubber sleeve

tungsten
putty

tungsten
putty

rubber
boom
sleeve

4oz Korda
Distance lead

Jon 'Shoes' Jones

'This rig has caught me loads of carp over the last few years. It's a rig I will always revert to if I start on a new water or visit waters in different countries. It's quite simple to tie: all you need is a Long Shank hook, an 8–10in length of strippable hooklink, some shrink tube, a lead and lead clip, followed by a 3ft looped tungsten leader.

'Strip the hooklink back to the required distance, then tie a loop to form the hair. Tie the hook on with a knotless knot making sure you leave a hair length of about two 14mm-baits' length from the bend. Cut two equal lengths of shrink tube of 12mm and one of about 3mm. Thread the

small piece on first followed by one of the longer lengths. Shrink them both down making sure the small piece is up along the shank and the longer one is covering the knot and is bent down at 45 degrees.

'Now slide the other length of shrink-tube over the top and repeat the process. This will stiffen up the shrink tube, creating better turning qualities. At the other end of the hooklink slide on a 30mm length of tubing to act as a boom, then tie on your swivel. Slide the tubing down over the swivel. All that is needed now is to add two or three blobs of tungsten to the hooklink to help it sit on the bottom better. I have found the best way to fish this rig is with a snowman presentation as bait.'

119

7 Staying One Step Ahead

BIG CARP BY DESIGN

Before I even start to delve into the depths of catching big fish, I'll make the point that I don't consider myself to be a Dave Lane or Terry Hearn. I have never set my sights on targeting only big fish, unlike Dave or Terry who are arguably two of Britain's finest. Obviously I love to catch the biggies, but I think dedicating your life and soul to these fish requires something that I don't have. I don't possess the patience required to consistently target the waters these lads tend to fish, most of which are relatively understocked with only a handful of biggish fish in them. I get bored very easily, which is possibly the main reason why I fish so many different venues.

Dave and Terry will tell you that big-fish anglers need to dedicate their time to a target water, something I have tried but not really enjoyed. In fact, I can only think of about a dozen or so waters that I have targeted throughout my carp fishing career. That's out of a total of over 350, 200-plus of which I have caught carp from. It is no surprise, therefore, that I have very few 'really big' fish under my belt. I have been fortunate the odd time, when I have caught a venue biggie, or one of the biggest, but I think I caught these through design – the use of a specific method suited to that type of water – as well as a bit of luck, rather than through my own patience and dedica-

tion. For a start, the types of water I tend to fish are those that I would consider to have a balanced level of stock, similar to those I think most of us fish, rather than those that require out-and-out dedication.

To begin this chapter I'd like to consider the topic of big carp by design, a term that has been given to the methods suited to the everyday carper who wishes to improve his chances of catching the bigger fish in a typically stocked type of carp venue. I'm not talking about the understocked Wraysburys or the Yateley Car Park Lakes of this world; I'm talking about your average day-ticket water where results with bigger fish can be largely dictated by the methods you use.

Big Carp – The 'Homies'

I shall look at methods for big fish in a moment, because first I wish to address possibly the most important topic (in my mind anyway) associated with big fish catching: that of location. Ask any big carp expert how important location is when it comes to big fish, and they will tell you very! The number of different venues I have fished where the bigger fish tend to get caught from the same area time and time again is amazing. I would say that over 75 per cent of the waters I have fished have possessed very territorial big fish, and this applies to ocean-sized reservoirs such as Raduta as well as small 3-acre waters like Withy Pool and includes even the small

The former world-record common of 76lb 7oz, with my good friend Christian
Finkelde, caught from a secret gravel pit in Germany.

A lone big fish rests in its favourite part of the lake, well away from the other fish.

World Record Bay at the famous Lake Raduta, once the home of the world-record mirror.

and very intricate waters. As a couple of examples, the world-record fish from Raduta only ever got caught from one area of the 2,500-acre (1,000ha) venue, a bay known as Record Bay. The same can be said of the Forest of Orient's biggie, known as The Bulldozer, which was only ever caught from Geradot bay. These two examples are both of large reservoirs, where I tend to think the biggies are more identifiably 'homies'. In England, it is sometimes harder to recognize territorial behaviour because the waters are much smaller and the swims are much closer to

Orchid Lake's Diana, a fish that certainly enjoyed visiting all areas of the lake.

one another, which can frequently lead to misinterpreted catch report details.

Unfortunately, big-fish catching is not always as easy as I have made it sound. There are also the venues where the biggies are travellers and get caught from all around the lake. Orchid Lake's big mirror known as Diana was one such fish. She was caught from all around the Oxfordshire venue, as indeed was Mary, the former British-record carp, which was caught from several different areas of Wraysbury. It therefore pays to learn a bit about your water before you set about fishing. There may not be any obvious information about the whereabouts of the biggies, but you may be able to piece together patterns of behaviour. Do the biggies tend to get caught from certain areas of the lake at certain times of the year? The Big 'Un in Motorway Pond certainly does. Does weather dictate where the biggies are caught from?

There will be waters where you can't do anything more than cross your fingers and hope for the best, but my initial line of attack when wishing to give myself a better chance of catching a biggie, or one of the biggies, is to do some research and try to fathom out where they generally get caught from. At least then I know that the odds are going to be slightly more in my favour. It is then just a matter of trying to increase them a bit more, and you can only do that through your method of presentation.

THE BAIT THEORIES

Big Baits

The first method I shall look at is very obviously the one that most anglers talk about when they think of trying to select bigger fish. The theory is that a bigger bait is harder to get into the mouth for a small fish. I know that a lot of continental anglers, such

Mini Grubber pellets are ideal for keeping the smaller carp occupied.

as the French, swear by this, but for me it has not always been successful. I recently caught a 1lb roach on a size 24mm boilie and that was during a session when I also caught two single-figure carp from a water that wasn't supposed to contain any! Nevertheless, despite the odd occasion when it isn't very successful, there are times when this method has worked. I tend to think that it is more suited to the type of water where there are large differences between the sizes of fish: the sort of place that has lots of doubles and singles and then a couple of really big fish, thirties or above.

Pool Hall in Wolverhampton used to contain only two or three thirties, one of which, named Humpy, made 37lb-plus. I'm going back to the early to mid-1990s now, but that place back then contained hundreds of small 4–8lb commons. It was the easiest venue in the world but, as you'd imagine, everyone who fished there went for Humpy or one of the other big commons. The number of times Humpy fell to big baits was unbeliev-

A large hookbait over the top of a bed of tiny baits: a good tactic on the right water.

You can fish multiples with all kinds of baits, from boilies to particles.

able. The method was to make hookbaits rock hard and over 30mm in size and bait profusely with small baits to attract the little 'uns into the swim. Some lads tried baiting with only big baits of 30mm and above, but this wasn't as successful as using the big baits over small ones. I think the tiny baits encouraged the small fish to select the baits they thought they could consume, leaving the big hookbait for the bigger fish.

Obviously, 30mm hookbaits are not the only size of bait you can use. I try to opt for a size that I think is relevant to my target water. The anglers at venues such as Chantecoq in France tend to use 40mm hookbaits, sometimes as high as 50mm, and feed the swim with copious amounts of 14mm and 18mm boilies. Here in England the way I like to do this is by feeding with tiny 8mm boilies or pellet and then presenting the larger hookbait over the top. I find this strategy is very much a match-type method because you have to

keep working and feeding the swim up if you want to increase your chances with the bigger fish. It doesn't work every time, and you may have to put up with the occasional nuisance little 'un, but if the method hasn't been flogged to death on your water I'd bet it would help you to single out the bigger fish eventually.

Multiple Hookbaits

This is another method based on the 'it's too big for the little fish' theory. I'm not a big fan of it, but I do know that it has a good track history with many anglers around the world. The theory is that you fish multiple hookbaits on the hair, like three 18mm or two 24mm, and so on, resulting in only the bigger fish being able to get the three or four hookbaits into the mouth. The reason it isn't one of my favourites is the number of times you get aborted takes on it. You end up getting the smaller fish picking up the outside baits only and not setting the hook, leaving you striking into nothing following a screaming take. If you do end up setting it, occasionally it is on the extreme outside of the mouth and sometimes in even worse positions.

Despite my reservations about using it, though, I have caught fairly well with multiple hookbaits. I used them at Raduta when I first fished there in 1998, banking my biggest common to date at 52lb. I know 52lb isn't a 'big' fish in a venue that contains carp of 82lb-plus, and many sixties and several seventies, but at the time I hadn't any

larger hookbaits with me and, when I used two or three grains, all I was catching was small twenties and grass carp. During the trip we lost some vital baggage on the flight over, including the bag that contained the big hookbaits, so my only option was to fish multiple hookbaits on a hair.

There are other times I have used it – on rivers in France, for example, as well as at a few day-ticket venues in the UK. I prefer using particles to boilies with the method, simply because I think that carp love to hoover when particles are in the swim, giving me more of a chance that one will pick

Carp angling legend Tim Paisley with a big common caught using a multiple bait hookbait.

A group of big carp battle it out to get to some bait in shallow water. I had been watching the fish visit the bait for over an hour before they started sampling.

up a large quantity of baits in one go. With boilies, especially the bigger sizes, I think they pick and choose – a 'here's one' type of feeding rather than a 'I must suck the lot up now'.

Whatever method I choose, though, I always favour a big hook like a size 2. I don't use anything smaller than this when fishing this method. I can't see any advantages in using a smaller hook. If a carp is going to pick up a multiple pile of bait, it is going to be sucking hard. A size 2 has a better chance of not only pricking but staying in.

Tactical Baiting and Hookbait Strategies

Of all of the methods I use for trying to select bigger fish, my favourite by far is through heavy baiting and then strategically placing my hookbaits among the free offerings. I'm a really big fan of the baiting pyramid, a method that Rod Hutchinson so expertly wrote about in *The Carp Strikes Back*. On the occasions I've watched groups of fish feeding on bait I have noticed that the more bait there is, the more carp will eventually come across it. Carp feeding activity stimulates other carp to investigate. I don't think they necessarily see or hear the other fish feeding and therefore visit and try for themselves, but I think they do communicate with one another, spreading the message that food is about. You only have to watch them to see this. You get one or two fish discover the food, try a bit, and then swim off. When they arrive back at the bait, some new fish are following them. Dick Walker once wrote that carp communicate by releasing hormones, which other fish sense, and I won't argue with this theory. As the new fish arrive, a feeding cycle

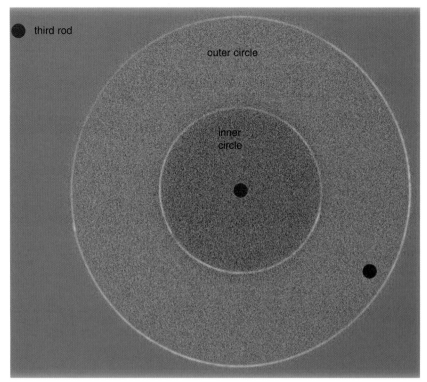

third rod

outer circle

inner circle

Tactcal baiting and hookbait strategy.

Inner circle: 400 boilies in a 3ft (1m) radius; single hookbait as free offerings.

Outer circle: 200 boilies in a 6½ft (2m) radius; hookbait as free offering.

Third rod: a four-bait stringer 6½ft (2m) past the outer circle; make the hookbait stand out – use a pop-up.

begins. Each fish takes a few, swims off, tells a few others, comes back, and the cycle starts again. In only a matter of minutes, on the right day, you can end up with several carp in the swim, all feeding.

My observations are that the bigger fish have a longer period feeding in the cycle than the others: the bigger the fish the greater the length of time it appears to spend taking its turn to feed. A small double will, say, spend 15 seconds, a twenty will spend a little bit longer, and so on. Obviously I'm generalizing when I write this, but the longer a fish stays in the feeding position the more food it is consuming. It therefore stands to reason that the more bait you put out at waters that are fairly well stocked, the greater your chances of catching a bigger fish.

Rather than just piling in the bait any old how, I actually try to take it to a further level, by trying to place it strategically. I try to bait with two different strategies rolled into one really: by having a very intensively baited area in the middle and a lightly baited area around the outside. I rate this method while fishing over silt with particles and I also rate it for selecting bigger fish.

I have already covered how I think bigger fish stay in the baited zone for longer periods than smaller fish, but I also think there are some big fish that are drawn to baited areas but will not feed heavily. Perhaps they will sample the odd item every now and again. Big fish haven't always achieved their size through being greedy. Some are cunning, some are even more cunning, and others are just out-and-out too cunning for anglers. This is where tactical hookbait placement comes in. I like to place my hookbaits around the baited zone in a way that gives me the best chance of catching a biggie. I place one right in the middle of the intensively baited area, aiming to select

One of my favourite captures, a 38lb lake record (at the time) mirror known as Curly Tail, taken from the very tough Brickyards fishery in East Yorkshire.

the lengthy feeder; I place one on the outside of all of the bait, aiming to select the cautious sampler: and there is also one on the outer ring of bait, to catch the really shy big fish.

Another hookbait strategy that has worked well for me is the use of a single hookbait. I am not just on about using this in the winter either. I use it at all times of the year and have had several venue biggies through its use. This method works well for those big fish that are loners. I think there are a lot of big fish like this, that just stay away from the hoards of other carp, even on the well stocked waters. A single hookbait may not look inviting to a shoal fish because it tends to prefer homing in on the big beds, whereas a lone biggie may be a scavenger (so to say) on the lookout for bits of food here and there. If you place one of these close to the area where a particular biggie tends to get caught, you may be doing yourself a favour. A lot of the time I fish three rods on the 'baiting pyramid' strategy and one on a single hookbait well away from where I think the majority of the fish are. It sounds daft, but it does work.

THE ATTRACTION OF SNAGS

Fallen trees, sunken boats, reed beds and similar features will always be a magnet for carp. Like so many different aspects of

129

Extreme fishing at Snagmere in South Africa – completely different to the snags we encountered at Lake Raduta.

Is your gear up to the job? The brutal tools needed to extract fish from Raduta's snags.

pursuing carp, though, fishing in snags requires a lot of thought, dedication and careful preparation. Indeed it is one of those topics that is not specific to a particular time of year, or one lake, so possibly the hardest thing to understand is how best to approach the situation you are confronted with. Snag fishing is risky, and the angler is always going to have to accept that pressured carp are two steps ahead of the mark.

I myself have experienced some horrendous snags in my time, both in England and overseas. The snags at Lake Raduta in Romania and at a venue I fished in South Africa (named Snagmere) are excellent examples of the extremities you may encounter in your carp careers. Raduta lies in a valley, and in the water are houses, street lamps, forests, churches – you name it, it's in the lake! These are coated with razor-sharp mussels, which tear even the toughest carp lines to bits. As for Snagmere, this venue is completely different to Raduta, in that the snags don't tear you up. At that venue, they lock you up solidly, which offers a completely different challenge in itself. Obviously you aren't likely to encounter snags like these on your local day-ticket water (or are you?), but the two venues serve as excellent examples of how one set of circumstances may need a very individual and specific line of attack. For Raduta I use 50lb mono leaders on 35lb braid; for Snagmere I used 15lb straight through.

Carp Welfare

Although all scenarios differ, and therefore tackle selection should too, there is one common factor that the angler should always bear in mind from snag to snag – and that is carp welfare. Whether it is your local pond with 5lb carp, or Conningbrook containing the British record, you need to use safe gear at all times and ensure that

One of three forties in a week from the snags at Raduta.

your fishing doesn't become a 'carp at any cost' pursuit.

In 1998 I was one of the first British anglers to experience Lake Raduta. On that occasion, the snags were somewhat more profuse than they are now (the owner has thinned them out). I was criticized by some high-profile anglers for tackling the lake with what some would class as horrendous gear. I'll accept any criticism where due, but I have always been an advocate for carp safety and many anglers who thought the need to have 'a pop' overlooked the fact that I was using barbless hooks. It was stated clearly in the features that I wrote at the time, and it is something I have since always felt the need to stress more obviously. Whether it is rig or tackle orientated, the

A big fish rests quietly amongst a set of snags.

first consideration has to be the welfare of the fish. These days, I tend to follow the barbless hook approach for most of my snag fishing, regardless of the strength of gear I'm using, basically because I have witnessed the damage that some rigs can do. At least with a barbless hook, the fish has a chance to free itself from a rig easier than it would from one with a whacking great barb attached to the hook.

Take it from me, and many other anglers who write in the mags, there is not as great a risk of losing fish with a barbless hook as folklore would have you believe. I have caught some superb carp using barbless hooks. I have lost fish I shouldn't have done with them, but then I have lost fish with barbed hooks, too.

Another area you should pay attention to is the line. Imagine receiving a pick-up, getting the fish totally snagged, and then having to pull for a break? When using a leader in this situation, the point where the line usually breaks is at the leader knot. This will result in the fish becoming snagged to the rig and a long length of leader if a barbed hook is being used, a set-up that may leave the fish stuck to a snag, weed bed or whatever. When using barbed hooks in snags always opt for a direct mainline and no leader. At least when pulling for a break with this gear, there is a greater chance that the swivel knot is where the line will part – resulting in the carp having only the rig in its mouth, which in most cases is lost fairly quickly.

Swim Selection

Another factor that affects carp welfare is swim selection. I don't mean getting in the swim where you can reach the snags, although this will quite obviously play a role in whether or not you catch. More specifically, I am talking about how to catch carp from the snags. A direct pull on a carp will put you in a better position for landing a fish than if the snag is tucked around the corner. Those that are directly opposite are best as they allow the angler to fish what is called 'locked-up'. Locked-up is when you fish with the bait-runner or drag system turned off, allowing no line at all to be pulled from the reel. The aim is to 'hit and hold' the carp and prevent it from reaching the sanctuary of the snags. It works wonderfully well so long as you sit on your rods and don't allow the carp a moment to bolt and gather momentum. A few extra moments is all it will take for the

carp to realize what is going on, causing it to bolt and, if you have a big fish hooked, applying too much pressure on the line and rod may cause the hook to pull or, worse still, the line to break. Make no bones about it, a big carp will snap even the most up-to-date carp line if it pulls suddenly and hard enough (and big carp can pull a lot harder than most anglers would believe!). I once waded out to a snagged carp at Motorway Pond in England. I got right next to the fish, touched it with the net, causing it to bolt, which in turn snapped my hooklink of 15lb. Even small carp can bolt hard so beware!

Fishing 'locked-up' is by far the best way of extracting carp from snaggy areas. The idea is to keep steady pressure on the fish,

Try to keep as direct a line as you can between the snags and your rod tips.

Tips on Locking Up

1. Where the bank allows, favour a bankstick set-up rather than a rod pod. If you are going to be fishing straight out in front of your swim, then a goalpost style set-up is ideal.

2. The emphasis is on getting an early indication, so if you are going to be fishing rods at an angle to one another, it would be better to disregard the goalposts in favour of single-leg banksticks so that you can point the rods directly at the hook-baits.

3. Ensure your buzzers are tight and are not able to twist out of position. Place one of the eyes of the rod right up against the buzzer head so that it acts as a wedge on the rod.

4. At the reel end, or butt section, of the rod, lock the rod to the banksticks using special butt grips. John Roberts and Rod Hutchinson make some excellent grips that can be used on a variety of set-ups.

5. Turn the bait-runner system on the reel to off and place the anti-reverse to on. Most modern-day carp reels are fitted with both of these settings.

6. Check the drag on the reel, setting it so that it isn't so tight that a heavy carp will snap the line, but not so loose that the fish will be capable of easily pulling some free. It's a kind of balancing act this, with experience helping you all the way.

7. I favour a tight-line presentation when fishing locked-up, almost so tight that the line is like a bow-string. I opt for light indicators of about 1oz in weight for distances of up to 100yd, choosing Solar's Re-coils or Fox's Swingers. Too heavy an indicator and it will give the fish too much margin for error.

Single banksticks are better than pods or buzzer bars as they allow you to keep a direct line on any obstacle.

Check the drag on the reel is at the correct setting.

8. Lastly, and very importantly, turn the vibration setting on the buzzer up as high as you can get away with. The setting should take into account the weather on the day and obviously not be so high that it gives you false registrations.

The set-up of the rods and indicators is as important as using the right bait and rigs.

not giving it an inch, unless you really do think something problematical is likely to occur (line parting, hook pulling, and so on). Let the rod's test curve and power extract the fish. Keep a good steady bend in the rod, remembering not to jerk it up and down, and try to retrieve line on the reel only when you feel you have the better of the fish. Rods are tools for landing fish, besides casting, so let it do its job. If you have to go to test curve then do so, but always allow some play in the rod so that the set-up has some 'give' just in case the fish gets the better of its senses. Steady pressure should put you in the driving seat. If, or should I say when, you get the better of the fish, depending on depth, you will probably see the fish or some boils on the surface. Keep the pressure on and don't give it an inch.

Locking up your gear may cause the fish to kite on the tight line created. This may take the fish around in an arc, which is why I prefer to fish directly opposite a snag rather than from the side. A fish kiting on a tight line still has an advantage over the angler if snags are also present to the side of where it was initially hooked. If it reaches the snag, there is a big chance there will be nothing you can do. Keep steady pressure on and try your best not to let the fish get buried within. If all becomes solid, then you will have only two or three options. One is to maintain steady pressure and wait until something happens. If after five or ten minutes everything is still solid, then I would release some of the pressure and place the rod back in the rest with the bail-arm off or bait-runner on. If the fish begins to move again, signalling so at the rod end, then immediately apply pressure once again. Hopefully this will put the angler back in control. If it doesn't then keep trying until it does. I have left a rod in this way for hours and landed the fish in the end so it pays to persevere. The only other two options are to pull for a break or try to free the fish. I never pull for a break until I am absolutely sure everything is lost. Usually I will leave a snagged rod as much as half a day before I decide all is lost. If the fishery allows I will take to a boat and at least try to free some of the line. Most of the time, snagged fish won't hang around for very long. They have a terrible habit of dropping the hook into a branch or similar once the tension has been released at their end. This is very frustrating and a very good reason

why you should always keep some sort of pressure on the line. Although I don't like going out to snagged fish from a boat, I will do it if I'm absolutely sure I've tried every other option available.

Baiting Principles

If you can't get in the swim – which offers you the best chances of landing fish – then look to the way you apply your bait as this can also assist your chances of catching

This one took twenty minutes to free from a snag 40ft (12m) below the boat.

from snags. Bait applied directly into the snag will probably send them further in. Conversely, bait applied on the edge will bring them out. Accurate baiting is vitally important when it comes to snag fishing. I can't stress this enough. Bait sprayed all over the place will help no one but the fish. I suppose this is one good reason for using bait boats. They offer advantages to the carp angler that no spod or throwing stick can ever do.

My favourite way of targeting snags is to place the hookbaits closer to the snag than the free offerings. This is a difficult area for me to address in print because I don't want to sound like I'm advising you to fish right on the edge of the snags. Far from it. Snags are usually very pressured areas of a lake, for obvious reasons. The ideal is to place the hookbaits as close to the snags as you can get away with. If the carp are not very difficult then you will probably be all right fishing the hookbaits on the furthest edge, but even the easiest of carp will soon begin to recognize they are better off selecting baits closest to the snag. This is where pre-baiting can help an awful lot, so if you are planning to fish a venue on a regular basis you won't go far wrong if you can apply a bit of bait every now and again.

Get 'Em Out of There!

The final consideration I want to cover is tackle selection. I tend to think that the hardest part of snag fishing is judging, or should I say knowing, which is the best tackle to use. When I say tackle here I mean line, leaders, hooks and hooklinks, and so on, not rods and reels. I mention the words judging and knowing there because you will find yourself doing both. On occasions, you will need to judge situations and calculate the best form of attack. This is when you are learning about the situation. The ideal is to reach a point where you are

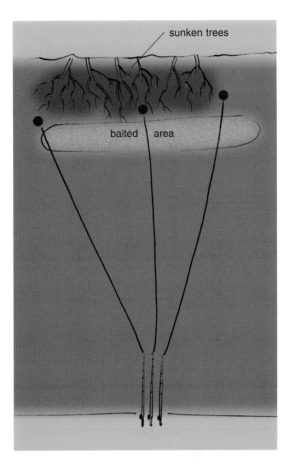

I like to place the hookbaits closer to the snag than I place the free offerings.

using the toughest tackle to withstand the snags, but also the lightest gear so that you are not making it too obvious to the carp.

To give you something to go on, these days I tend not to use more than two types of hook for my fishing. This includes my overseas fishing as well as my English. The last ten years I have been using the Precision and Grippa hooks by Rod Hutchinson. Both are superbly sharp and will cover all the needs of any angler. I'm not talking from the commercial side here either. Yes, I did work for Hutchy, but people who read my articles regularly will know that I didn't plug all of his gear and I did plug other companies. I try to keep the commercial side of carp fishing out of my writing and plug only the gear that I use and can recommend. Rod's hooks are superb. The Grippa hooks are fairly springy when compared to the Precision. I tend to use the Grippa for simple to moderate snag fishing, such as when I'm fishing up against reeds or single sunken branches. Where I need to really step things up, I favour the Precision. These are excellent for overseas venues where you need to keep heavy pressure on big fish and know that the pattern is capable of staying in and not opening out. Have a look at them both. There are of course several other excellent patterns available, so shop around and see which suit your style. Look for hooks with a fairly heavy wire and small shank.

The one area that probably needs more attention than all others when it comes to tackle is line. Line selection needs to be based on toughness more so than suppleness, unless that is, you will be required to cast long range to reach the snags – in which case you will need to balance things out. Snags are the ideal place for sharp mussels to attach themselves so, to prevent cut-offs, make sure you are using a hard-wearing line. This seems obvious, but the number of anglers I see or hear about using feeble lines in snags just goes to show that

people are prepared to sacrifice strength for pick-ups. I've no idea why anglers follow that line of attack; my view is that it is much better to have only one pick-up and a landed fish than four pick-ups and none on the bank. I'm of the opinion that a lost carp is not only a disappointment at that particular moment, but that it also has a bearing on whether or not you will actually catch one in that session.

Line is a personal thing so I won't even mention which brands I use. I'll just say that I don't use pre-stretched lines in snags and I only use monos. Monos are much tougher on a pound-for-pound basis than braids. I carried out some tests before I went to Raduta a few years ago. At the time I was being led a song and dance by the marketing of some braids and believed braids were tougher than monos. When I carried out the tests I realized that the marketing was wrong in most cases. The only negative thing is that heavy monos can be twisty, although I'll gladly put up with a bit of that if it means a better chance of landing a carp. The only positive side I can see to braids is that they have very little stretch and so register pick-ups a lot better and don't give the carp an inch.

There you have it then. That's a look at a few of my opinions on how best to approach snag fishing. Other anglers may

For snag fishing, Grippa hooks are as good as it gets.

Line. It's a personal thing, but you'll need a tough one for most snaggy situations.

Weed. Don't be afraid of it!

tell you a different way of doing it, and indeed they may be right for the occasion they/you are fishing. No snags are the same. No situations are the same. Keep an open mind at all times and try to work out how best to extract the carp. There are no shortcuts. Some say it is a science, and I wouldn't argue that it isn't.

WEEDED-UP FISH

It is inevitable that regular carpers will come across a situation that involves fishing amongst beds of weed. Come the months of July and August, the carp just love to soak up the sun cruising around weed where an abundance of natural food will also be available. Certainly on some of the waters I've fished, the carp spend hours with their backs out of the water almost oblivious to the leads and marker floats landing around them as they pick at the snails and crustaceans clinging to the blooms and stems. Weed, however, has a habit of beating a lot of anglers mentally, with plenty of fish lost through bad tactics.

One of the venues I fish, Tilery Lake in East Yorkshire, is very rich, with blanket weed all over the bottom. On the bars, which run in several places up and down the lake, there is also stringy weed from top to bottom. A thirty-plus I once caught from the venue took me about seven hours to land as I had to extract it from several weed beds. The hardest ones were obviously the long-range ones since the stretch in the line meant that most of the power in the rod was lost, even at full compression. I don't like walking backwards with the rod flat when using monofilament because I can't monitor the power as well as I can with the rod hooped over my shoulder. If the rod is at test curve and nothing is shifting out at the business end, that is the sign for me to put it back in the rest and leave it. Carp that are in weed are there because they feel safe, and experience has told me that there is only one way a long-range carp is going to come out of a weed bed and that is of its own accord.

It is all too easy to think that when a carp has become weeded up the best thing to do is pull for a break. The weed at Tilery, as an example, really does cause carp to become snagged up solid. It is top to bottom in sev-

eral areas and when fishing close to it I have found that the best thing to do is to keep winding and heaving as much as you can. If it does find the weed, then this is when you have to tell it that you have gone. I have tried several methods of trying to coax them out, and I think the best thing to do is to knock the bail-arm over and leave the line free-running and wait: and I mean wait! Bait-runners have resistance on the line and I tend to think that weeded-up carp can even identify whether you've gone or not by

A 30lb 12oz mirror from Tilery Lake in East Yorkshire, a venue full of weed.

With a bit of patience, you can get them out of there quite easily.

the smallest amount of resistance exerted by these. The rig may still be in the carp's mouth, but I don't think that is what they are so concerned about. It is the 'being pulled' that bothers them most: the fact that they are not going where they want to – it kind of panics them.

I left one fish in weed for over three hours before it started to move. I knocked the bail-arm off as soon as the carp became solid, then placed the rod back in the rest and made a cup of tea. I was glad I did since the carp ended up being over 30lb when I eventually landed it after extracting it from several thick beds of weed.

It isn't something that works every single time I get a weeded-up fish, but I can honestly say that in all of the years I have been

carp fishing this method has proved to be the best by far. I think I have an 80 per cent chance of landing a carp that has become weeded up if I knock the bail-arm off and wait. Sometimes the carp are so cute they just shed the hook as soon as they reach the weed, but if I had to give any advice on this one it would always be to wait and be patient: never just give it a couple of minutes before you pull for a break.

As a final example of why you should wait, let me tell you about a fish that one of the other Tilery anglers caught while I was on the lake. Neil Harrison had been fishing one of the swims just down from me and had finished his twenty-four-hour session with five carp. As he left he popped in to see me and tell me about what he'd

Battling a big mirror through weed at Motorway Pond. Keep a tight line on them at all times, and they will come. (Photo: Geoff Thomson)

caught. I'd sat in my swim for forty-eight hours for only one fish so, as you would, I jumped into his swim behind him. It was probably about half an hour after he left that I went into his swim, and I'd probably been there about ten minutes before I stepped onto the board and had a look in the margins at my feet. About a rod-length out was an upper-twenty mirror just sat in the weed. It didn't bolt when it saw me, but eventually glided off after about fifteen minutes. I later found out that an hour before Neil left he'd returned a fish that he'd just landed. He told me it was sulking in the weed when he left. It swam off well, but went straight into a weed bed and stayed there. It was obviously the same fish, and had been in the same position for over two hours at the very least.

Lead Attachments for Weed

Kevin Nash wrote some very informative articles many years ago about how dumping the lead when weed fishing would give the angler more of a chance of landing a

fish. In my opinion, Kevin was exactly right, with any fixing on the line, no matter how small – even a size 10 swivel – leaving the angler open to a build-up of weed that continues to amass the further one pulls through it. As the first strand gets stuck, another one grabs hold, then another, until eventually you are attached to a great big ball of the stuff which will put the line under so much stress that only the patient type will maintain any chance of landing a fish.

Dumping the lead is the perfect way to fish any type of weedy water since the bigger a fixing is, the more chance it has of picking up any unwanted 'washing'. However, in today's 'green' environment where anglers themselves are quick to have a pop at others for advocating certain methods I think it's always wise to keep angling in the right light and away from any negative press. You only have to go on the carp fishing websites to see what I mean by that statement, because all hell seemed to break loose when some top-name anglers wrote a piece about dumping several dozen leads in a lake to get on top of the fish. Despite there being a world of difference between insoluble and soluble lead, though, I still think it is important that anglers keep things as positive as they can, and it is for this reason that I generally don't 'lead dump' unless there is no alternative way of tackling a situation. Even then, I will only dump one or two.

An In-Line Fan

I tend to favour – first and foremost – in-line leads for weed. My current set-up for either Motorway Pond or the extremely weedy Tilery Lake is to use a heavy 5oz Armaled in-line. Although they do get 'bulked-up' with washing every now and again, more so in heavy Canadian pondweed, I still find an in-line presentation less prone to bulking than a lead clip combined with a free dangling lead system, even the type that are designed to shed the lead should a fish become weeded. Over the last two years I have landed all but one of the fish I have hooked in weed. One or two of these have become weeded for quite some time, but it is my opinion that it has been the fish rather than the lead that has caused this to happen – the fish diving for cover once it sees it has a chance. Had it been anything different, such as the lead becoming locked up, I don't think I would have landed them, with perhaps the hooklink parting at the swivel as the fish tried to free itself from the obstruction.

With the production of ready-made rig kits, instructional videos and step-by-step type magazines, I believe that some of the newer carp anglers are overlooking the benefits of using in-line leads in weed as they become almost preoccupied with the use of lead clips. The original concept of a lead clip was to protect the line nearest to the swivel when an angler was going for a big cast, but the almost blanket coverage of

Washing on the line, indicating that the lead attachment being used is not really suited to the situation.

them has made many people more focused on fashion than on real success as carp anglers. In 2003 at least two anglers had to call the *Carp-Talk* office so that Kev Clifford could go and free weeded fish at Motorway Pond (less than a mile down the road from the office), on both occasions 20lb-plus carp that had become tethered on lead clips that had slipped down the

Big-carp catcher Steve Briggs with a 40lb-plus common from the weed bed visible just over his shoulder.

line. Basically, what happened was that as the fish powered off, the clips, accompanied by the lead, had come free from the swivel, almost staying in exactly the same position as they were when cast, whilst the fish wove itself into a complete mess wrapping itself around and around the weed until it couldn't move any more. The brilliant Lockjaw clip by Armaled, which grips the swivel, was designed to prevent this problem, proving itself to be the best on the market, even helping to shed the lead from the clip fairly easily when the fish powers off – a smooth-fitting tail rubber helping this to happen. However, the point

I'm trying to make is that even this system won't be as effective as an in-line if the angler chooses to fish in the sensible way of locking up his gear, a method advocated by all and sundry.

Fishing locked up with the bait-runners turned off and everything as rock-solid as we can make it puts the angler in so much control when weed is around that only a brave or unaware angler would choose to fish another way. Imagine what a lead dangling from the line, or clip, would do to a locked-up set-up. It would defeat the object of trying to stay in control and in my mind just ask for trouble. Think about what hap-

In-lines, my first choice for weed.

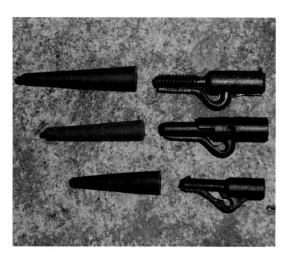

Lead clips: good or bad for weed?

pens in a fight. Let's imagine the angler is pulling in a fish, which is like a dead weight. With a clip and swivel lead, the lead would be pulled away from the tail-rubber opening and forced against the thick section of the clip, making it a much bulkier item than a streamlined in-line. As I've said , even an in-line will not put a stop to bulking up but the more streamlined a terminal set-up is the better the chances for the angler.

Despite the safety clip's ability to free the lead if the fish pulls in the opposite direction, I just don't want that to happen when obstructions are around, hence my always choosing in-lines ahead of all others. I don't know about the rest of you, but I prefer to be the one in control when battling in weed, gaining as much line as I possibly can, as quickly as I can. I know from speaking to some of the lead manufacturers that in-lines don't sell as well as Distance/Zipp-type leads, but that doesn't mean there isn't a place for them in every angler's armoury. They may not be an in-vogue piece of kit, but they will do the job that is required – even more so if the angler also possesses a bit of patience should a fish become stuck in weed.

CLIPS FOR BAGGING

The topic of lead attachments brings me nicely onto the topic of lead clips for PVA bagging. Without wanting to sound like I don't advocate the use of lead clips (which is far from the truth), I'd like to point out another scenario when certain brands don't recommend themselves to the carp angler.

Courtesy of Boyer Leisure I paid a visit to Colnebrook West in the Colne Valley in 2003 for a couple of nights. It was a spur-of-the-moment visit that saw me fishing with PVA bags using a mixture of pellets and air-dried Addicted Mix, which I'd crumbed up with a pair of pliers. I ended up with a four-fish catch, one lost – and I wasn't doing anything special with the bags I was using. I used the Kryston Melt-Ex variety, which I really like, placing the hookbait in first (a red MC Mix/ Addicted pop-up), and then covering this with the pellet and the broken boilie. The lead was the last thing to go in, and the whole lot was fastened with a piece of PVA tape at the top, with the excess doubled back on itself. I use this particular set-up

A mid-twenty leather from the very weedy Tilery Lake, when an in-line lead served its purpose well.

A summer's day at Colnebrook West in the Colne Valley.

because I much prefer my hookbait to sit on top of the lead and the feed when it reaches the bottom; this is why I place it into the bag first. The bag will obviously fall through the water weight end down, the freebaits covering this and the hookbait resting right on top in pole position. I've used this method for what seems like ages and I haven't found a venue that it doesn't work on.

I don't know what the rest of you like when it comes to choosing lead for PVA bags, but I probably use the model that needs sliding onto a lead clip the most (apart from in very thick weed), basically because the bulk of the clip and lead offers a better fixing for sealing the PVA bag. Usually the tie goes around the area where the lead attaches to the clip, with the bulk of the lead resting below in the bag.

My favoured PVA bag presentation, with the top fastened with a strip of PVA tape, the excess doubled back over the top.

147

I have been a fan of the Korda clips with the serrated edge for what seems like ages now, but at Colnebrook West I thought I'd give the Nash continental type (without teeth) a go to see how well they performed. I don't want to start a war here, but the first half a dozen times I used these clips in bags I ended up with a couple of situations where the bag hit the water and, as soon as I tried to tighten up, the lead came free from the rig. What's that all about? I thought to myself. On closer inspection I noticed that the type of clip I was using had no teeth on the clip arm, so it was extremely easy for the silicon sleeve to come free and therefore the lead to slip off. At Colnebrook I quickly rectified the problem, but I then went on to Oxlease Lake at Richworth Linear for a junior event and noticed two other anglers (one senior) encountering the same problem when using the Armaled type of clip (also with no teeth on the clip). The bag was cast out, it dissolved, and within a matter of seconds the lead had come free. Both anglers were using the same clips that haven't any teeth on the main housing – exactly the same as the Nash Continental ones.

How this particular problem occurs I can't really explain because I was never

A nice common from Colnebrook West. It was during this session that the problems with clips and bags first came to light.

Korda's clips, my first choice clip for
PVA bagging.

very good at physics. The only thing I can
think is that with the force of the cast, or
the bag hitting the water, there is so much
pressure applied on the silicon sleeve
(where the bag is tied) that it pushes it
upwards from the clip. I was lobbing the
bags out at Colnebrook only about 40yd
(35m) or so, so it doesn't appear to happen
only with heavy casting.

I'm pretty sure that both Nashy and
Armaled have designed their clips for
something other than PVA bagging, such as
fish welfare, so it isn't an oversight on their
part. My point is: make sure you are aware
of this so that you can avoid it. I believe the
method of tying the top of a bag with some
PVA string and using it with a clip is the
most widely used – simply because the bulk
of the lead is the ideal holding position for
the tie at the neck.

The only way around this problem is
either to use a Korda clip with the teeth on,
or to make sure that once you have placed
the lead into the bag you cover it with
enough free bait so that the clip is well
below where you tie the bag together. Be
careful, though, because if you use only a
single-skinned bag or one that isn't very
tightly compacted, the clip may force its
way through the freebait and towards the

opening. This is especially likely to happen
when going for a long chuck. You can
reduce the chances of this by giving the
sides of the bag some extra stability by doubling it back over the sides – as if you were
placing a condom over your real end tackle! – or by compacting the top freebait so
much that it just cannot budge out of place.

I have not noticed this problem when
using the toothless clips without the bags
(such as casting a single hookbait on the
Nash or the Armaled one), so I am convinced it is something specific to bagging.

DON'T NEGLECT
THE MARGINS

It has been said a million times before, but
how many of us still neglect the margins? I
for one have been through plenty of stages
in my carp fishing career when I've totally
overlooked the areas closest to the bank,
both those at my feet and on the opposite
side. It's all so easy to think that the carp
will be browsing the areas out in the middle of the lake where they can escape the
noise and presence of humans, but even at
the most pressured of venues you can guarantee that if the time is right they will be
found very close in.

While carp will browse the margins at
any time of the year, I myself have had
some excellent success close in during the
height of summer, although to be fair you
may experience good results at any time of
the year. When the temperatures are high,
and especially in the early hours of the
morning when noise is likely to be almost
non-existent, they love to come browsing
the areas of the lake where they might not
otherwise go in the middle of the day. If
you are fishing a venue that also allows
match and pleasure anglers to cast a line,
the carp will know all about the patches of
ground bait, maggots and sweet corn that

149

An ideal margin spot offering lots of cover for the fish.

will have been thrown in when the day anglers depart. They will also know about the freebies thrown in by carp anglers when, for example, they take off an old hookbait and lob it into the margins. It is also where they will find a healthy supply of grubs, such as caterpillars and flies, which will have fallen in from the overhanging trees.

Finding success through fishing in the margins, however, requires its own little touches by the angler.

Slack Lining

I don't think there's any need for me to go into great lengths about how keeping quiet when fishing close in will enhance your results. It has been written about so many times in the past, I bet most of you are bored with reading about it. Instead, I think it is more important to talk about getting the set-up right, especially when it comes to the lie of the line and the positioning of the rods.

Make no bones about it, a tight line close in to the bank is something that the carp will spook off very easily if they are used to seeing anglers in the area where the baits are being presented. Even in the dark, they will be aware of the line, especially if it is so tight it is transmitting sound vibrations down it.

These days I tend to opt for slack lining when fishing close in to the margins at my feet, especially if I'm right underneath the rod tips. I've been doing it for probably ten years now, since talking to Kevin Nash about it whilst he was fishing in this way at Warmwell. Although I had known about the advantages of slack lining for many years, at first I didn't like the idea of my set-up not recording an indication as soon as the fish had picked up the bait (something that you tend to get with a tight line). However, once you've caught a few fish by doing it, you begin to realize that fish hooked when slack lining tend not to know they have been hooked until they feel

Cloud city. You could say the fish are going a bit potty for the bait in this marginal swim.

resistance on the line, even when dragging a heavy lead around with them.

I like to create as much of a bow in the line as I can when fishing like this, sometimes even offering a light back lead between the tip and the rig just to keep the line out of harm's way (just in case you get a margin browser wrapped up in all the line). There's no need for indicators with this set-up, just the buzzers set fairly high on the sensitivity front. At first a take may appear rather twitchy, but as soon as the fish knows it is hooked you'll know about it!

Fish hooked close in under your feet tend to go off like steam trains when they know something is trying to pull them in, and this is the reason I always fish my bait-runners fairly loose in this situation. A big carp hooked close in will be capable of pulling a rod off the rest very easily if the clutch is set too tight. It's a balancing act really, because you don't want it so loose that when one powers off you are left with a bird's nest of line wrapped around the reel.

Solar's indicators are brilliant for slack lining.

A fat common of almost 30lb from Birch Grove in Shropshire, taken on a slack line close in to the margins.

Fish hooked close in go off like rockets when they know the battle has commenced!

Far Margins

Certainly at the beginning of my campaign on Motorway in 2005 I found a lot of success by fishing tight in to a far margin. Opposite the swim known as Danny's Point there is a small bay that doesn't allow fishing off that bank – a bay that has the perfect carp attractors in reeds, the odd snag and a small set of lilies. The distance is all of about 100yd (90m) maximum, and with a snappy cast even into a head wind I wouldn't say it is a tricky one unless you want to be as tight as you possibly can.

With the swim having been fished hard for many years, it didn't take long for the fishing to get harder once I'd taken my first few fish from the spot. This was where pin-point hookbait placement really came in, and where a bait boat started to show its

Danny's Point at Motorway Pond, where one of the hot spots is tight to the far bank.

worth in my fishing. After a couple of weeks the carp would only pick hookbaits up that were fished as tight as I could possibly get to a set of reeds. It was so close, in fact, that I was needing a pair of binoculars to get my baits into the position that I needed them, which was perhaps only a couple of inches off the stems.

With 100yd (90m) of line out and only inches to play with, it was essential that my gear was locked up as solid as I could get it. I was using one of Rod Hutchinson's stainless pods, which although fairly heavy played the perfect roll in keeping my rods in a solid position. Combined with some John Roberts Butt Grips, my bait-runners switched off with the drag set high, as tight a line as I could get it, and my Solar Re-Coil indicators loaded up with only a slight dip in the line, it was a mere single bleep

that was making me bolt from the bivvy and onto the rods.

With the rods pointing directly at the hookbaits, at that sort of distance I sometimes find it hard to detemine whether or not a single bleep is a take, so one of the things I do is point the rods down into the water so that the tips are just below the surface, with there being a slight angle created downwards in the pathway of the line at the point of the rod tip. I will ensure that everything is as level as I can possibly get it on the set-up, even to the point of ensuring that each tip is sunk at exactly the same depth.

What tends to happen when something pulls on the other end when fishing in this way is that the tip will be raised higher than the others. The first bleep is the sign to go and investigate. If the rod that has

153

Dip the tips just below the surface of the water to help you identify when something is on the other end.

received the bleep has its tip slightly raised, it's game on!

This is where hook-and-hold tactics really take over because you can't afford to give a fish an inch when fishing so tight to a far margin. In 2005 I was using the Intrigue rods by Hutchy, which, compared to the Dream Makers that I'd used for quite some time, were quite soft. My second take from Danny's Point at Motorway got the better of me, but come the end of the season, once I'd got used to them, I'd lost only two fish to the snags, which wasn't bad when you consider I landed twenty-nine from there!

THE RE-CAST STRATEGY

Earlier in the book I touched on how carp can single out hookbaits and mark them as dangerous. At venues where they depend on anglers' bait to survive, I'm convinced that they quickly home in on any food items that are introduced. The longer a period of time goes by without any action at this type of water therefore, the more I would be convinced that my hookbaits had been singled out and marked.

There are so many occasions when I have turned a quiet period of fishing into action simply by re-casting one of my rods. By this statement I'm not on about re-casting to a showing fish either, more just a re-positioning of the hookbait or freshening up of the freebaits around it. The bait won't necessarily need to be moved by any great distance, firing it back out to exactly the same spot and trying to confuse the carp into thinking that everything in the swim has changed – a sort of game really, asking the carp to take a chance once again.

Some of the best examples I have seen of this type of approach working well have been during the carp fishing matches I've participated in. Usually, these sorts of event are held at the waters that have a fairly high stocking density, waters where the carp are more willing to take the hook-bait challenge. The competitive nature of some of the anglers has led many into knowing exactly when a hookbait has been singled out and needs redoing. Most of the time I know I've been sussed by the fish if I have received a single bleep on the buzzer followed by a slight drop-back. Obviously hitting the rod as quick as I possibly can sometimes catches the fish off guard, but most of the time we are too slow, and as

soon as the drop-back has registered it's time to readjust things.

Other times when I know things need adjusting is when lengthy periods of time have passed between casting out and nothing happening. A lot of anglers have a habit of baiting up and doing their rods at exactly the same time each day – just before dark and as soon as they get up, usually a couple of hours into daylight. This sort of approach may lend itself well to some waters, but you can bet your bottom dollar

Success from Danny's Point with a 30lb 10oz mirror that gave only a single bleep on the indicator.

Time for a re-cast?

First light is a great
time for the re-cast
strategy, especially
during the spring
and summer months.

that at the trickier venues it will get sussed every time. Before I got my night ticket for Motorway Pond in East Yorkshire, I spent several years fishing the place on the day book, which allowed anglers on the fishery from five in the morning until ten at night. I can tell you that arriving at a water for 5 a.m. is a real eye-opener. Everyone who has been night fishing is usually tucked up in bed totally oblivious to what is happening. Baits have usually been out since just before dark the previous evening and the anglers have no intention of moving unless a carp signals a pick-up.

In the summer months, however, a fresh pile of bait in a feeding area didn't seem to fail, and within a couple of hours of arriving good catches were regularly made by the day-permit holders. I thought the early

A fresh pile of bait is sometimes just the job on the pressured waters.

A brace of superb mid-thirties for Rob Hughes and me in South Africa, when rising early enabled us to take advantage of an important feeding spell at Klaserie Dam.

Hookbaits left out all night at venues where nuisance species are in abundance may get whittled down to nothing.

morning re-cast was something specific to Motorway, until I took the same strategy to other waters and found that I also caught well from venues such as Birch Grove, Orchid Lake and Tilery Lake. I also used it at South Africa's Klaserie Dam the very first time I went to that country. I'll admit that I was catching carp in the dark at Klaserie, but I'm convinced that had I not risen at first light and re-cast, I wouldn't have caught as many fish as I did. Rob Hughes was fishing with me at the time, and we both ended up rising every morning at first light to re-cast. On one particular morning, we had six takes between 5 and 8 a.m. resulting in three fish over 40lb and a further two over 34lb whilst nothing else was caught from the lake.

I have since used the early morning re-cast strategy on several other occasions and experienced similar results. Another great example was during the qualifying rounds of the 2000 British Carp Angling Championships at Tyram Hall in Yorkshire. Tim Paisley was my partner and we were getting up for first light and baiting up and re-casting. We were up for 5.30 both mornings during the forty-eight-hour event and had finished baiting and re-casting all rods

within twenty minutes. Action followed within the hour whilst all the other anglers were still asleep and unaware of the feeding actions of the fish. We went on to a convincing win in the match.

Whilst I have tried the re-cast strategy at all other times of the day and night to great success, the first light cast always seems to be the most obviously effective. I'm still not exactly sure why this is so. Maybe baited areas that have been left out all night have been whittled down by nuisance fish. Maybe they have lost their attraction, or maybe they have become masked or coated in deposits that they are just not as attractive or obvious to the fish. It works, though, and it works exceedingly well if you are the first on a water to do it regularly. I know of venues that are renowned for being night-only waters and then all of a sudden become better morning waters through re-casting at first light.

Have They Moved?

Ever been in one of those situations when you are hauling fish at a water and all of a sudden the action stops? Nine times out of ten you will blame it on the fish moving out, but nine times out of ten they will simply have lost confidence in where you have been hooking them, marking the area rather than the hookbait.

This theory is an extension of the re-cast strategy and is best explained by giving you an example of one incident that occurred when Steve Briggs and I were fishing at Lake Raduta in Romania. During 2002 we spent two weeks fishing a huge area of water that gave us a host of different options. It was at the dam end of the lake. We had no one around us and together we probably had about 500 acres (200ha) of water to ourselves. I had the most action in the first week of the trip, catching three fish between 40lb and 48lb 8oz out of ten takes whilst

Steve had only three fish to 22lb. I was at the right-hand side of the swim and out in front of us we had an old river bed with sunken trees and bits of debris littering its length. This stretched right the way from my right all the way past Steve's swim.

At the end of the first week, I'd had good-sized fish from both of my spots (I had two rods in each area). There hadn't been any sort of pattern to which rod went – the fish were just out in front of me. As is always the case when you have some going spots in your swim, I kept the bait going out in these areas and kept placing the hookbaits out to the spots that had produced fish – something that we all do instinctively. By this time, Steve was really pulling his hair out because he just couldn't buy a biggie or much action from his side of the swim. His right-hand rod was creeping ever so close to my left, and by the halfway stage I

told him to get it as close as he could to my area, which ended up being about 5yd away – he couldn't get it any closer because a snag blocked his path. I was using a blend of Hutchy's MC Mix with Addicted over the top of Haiths mixed seed and at the same time he also changed his bait over to this.

The next twenty-four hours changed the picture completely. The action dried up in my swim whilst it picked up for Steve. I was sitting there watching exactly what Steve had been watching the week earlier. All of the better fish came from in front of him, within a range of 10yd from my left-hand marker. It was obvious that they'd moved ever so slightly to my left, which, if Steve hadn't been there, was still within my area of water. By the end of the second week, Steve was smiling as much as I'd been and collectively we had landed

Raduta in freezing cold conditions during the October 2002 session.

One of the forties from the right-hand side of the swim during the first week of the trip.

Steve moved over to the same baiting pattern as well as moving his rods closer to where I'd been catching.

six fish over 40lb, three of which were over 45lb. Had I been in the swim all by myself, I honestly don't believe that I'd know what I do now. If I think back to the times that the action has dried up in front of me whilst fishing alone and, instead of just trying a few different spots within my swim and close to the areas that I've had pick-ups from in the past, I have simply packed up and moved on in the belief that the fish have moved out.

I know that I'm not alone here either, since most of my friends, including anglers of the calibre of Tim Paisley, Rod Hutchinson and Steve, mentioned the same to me when we returned from this trip. Virtually all of us do it. We just pack up and move on, instead of considering that the fish

The first decent one for Steve, a 46lb common from the left-hand side of the swim,
only yards from where I'd been catching.

may be only a few yards away and still very catchable. Steve, in fact, decided to put this theory to the test during his next winter trip to Lac de St Cassien. When the action dried up from his original spots, he moved the hookbaits around the swim rather than move out. It worked a treat for him, and having since taken this same strategy to several other waters I'm convinced that we can all extend the action in our swims by just tracking down new areas to re-position hookbaits.

I think carp can be very isolated at times, and once they've tracked down an area of bait they will stay very close to it for several days, even if they don't appear to be feeding on it. I'm not just on about big

waters here: I firmly believe that carp in small UK waters act in the same way. The results from this trip really did make me think, and during one summer I suspected this same thing was happening to me at Tilery Lake in East Yorkshire. There was one particular session when I had a great two days during a three-day stint. The third day it really did dry up leaving me with the thought that I'd hammered them out of the swim. I was back at the lake a couple of days later, in the same swim, with the first day being a blank. At first I thought I'd made a mistake opting for the same swim, but on the second night I had a bream at about 2 a.m. from one of the areas I had caught from the week earlier. I

Another big common comes Steve's way, indicating that the fish had moved ever so slightly towards his side of the swim.

couldn't be bothered to set up the bait boat and spend twenty minutes getting it exactly right, so I cast a stringer as hard as I could in the general direction of where I'd been fishing. It landed somewhat short of the mark (about 10yd or so because I could tell from the mark I had on my line). A couple of hours later I was woken to a screamer on that rod which turned out to be a low twenty. I put the same rod back out and a short while later it again produced a take. I continued to fish this particular spot for the remainder of the trip and ended up pulling a couple of nice fish from it, indicating to me that the fish had perhaps been spooked from the first spots but were still very close by.

I suspect that all too often we all fall foul of the sneaky movements of the carp, even when we think we are on top of them. Re-casting a hookbait to a new area or simply just re-positioning one, however, can make the big difference between catching and blanking. A lot of anglers go fishing to escape the day-to-day pressures of work so are happy to sleep through the early morning feeding spell I mentioned earlier, or are happy to endure motionless indicators while they chill out. To a lot of anglers, though, doing nothing to increase your chances of catching carp just defeats the object of being there. You may as well try while you are there, otherwise you may find that the only activity you are participating in is the netting and photographing of the fish for your mate!

FISHING OVER SILT

Few would disagree with the view that silt offers a great deal of carp catching potential. Being light enough to house all sorts of crustaceans and goodies like bloodworm, very few areas of silt slip by unnoticed by the carp. You can almost guarantee that if there's silt in your water the carp will know about it and probably feed there. The only drawback is that where it is few and far between compared to the surrounding bottom, it is sure to be very obvious to the angler as well, putting the fish very much on guard and under pressure. On the other hand, however, where silt is abundant the task of locating the feeding areas is more difficult. In fact, it can be so difficult at times that this is one of my main reasons for labelling the silty meres and estate lakes

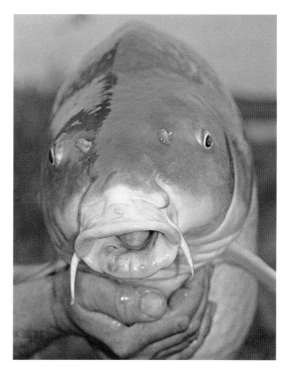

How often do we fall foul to the sneaky movements of the carp?

The Mangrove Swamp in Shropshire, home of some very tricky carp.

This slow meandering river is also likely to have its fair share of silt areas, especially where sets of pads have established.

that are found all over the country as being some of the hardest venues to fish.

Getting to know the lake bed is where success at silt fishing really lies, especially on those waters that possess a great deal of it. I'm not trying to degrade any capture of carp, but I firmly believe that not even the pressure cycle can make some gravel pits as hard as the silty meres or estate lakes. Stocking density aside, on an average basis, silty meres and estate lakes just have an awkward nature about them. When you feel that you've got the better of their carp,

something changes as if a switch has been flicked, and you find yourself starting right back at square one. I'd even go as far as to say that the meres and the estate lakes are two different scenarios in themselves. You only have to consider the nature of them to see this. The meres are usually a lot deeper than the estate lakes, and normally devoid of bottom weed apart from the odd set of lily pads around marginal shelves. Ihe middle of the mere silt deposits are usually abundant, having built up over many years or even centuries. Springs force their way through the mere bed, and many appear to lose their carp to the depths and wilderness that many estate lakes don't have. Estate waters are much different, usually having a dam of some sort. Depth is normally greater here, and this will gradually slope away towards the inlet end. Weed and pads will be found in many areas, with the only similarities between the two types of water being the feeder stream and outlet, and, of course, the abundance of silt – silt that ranges in depth from fractions of an inch to as much as several feet; silt that has built up after years and years of leaf matter falling from the trees that surround the banks or neighbouring water courses.

It isn't just the silty meres and estate waters that provide anglers with silt. Silt can be found in all other forms of water, be they sand pits, clay pits, gravel pits, canals or river systems. Depending on the age of the water as well as its location, the depths and abundance of the silt found in these venues is usually very different. Exceptions are usually the meres and estate lakes, which are old and often unmanaged.

So, apart from the abundance of it, what is it about silt that makes venues so unique? Why do carp love the stuff on some waters and appear to completely avoid it on others? More to the point, why do anglers need to be armed with a variety of different methods

This nice-looking 30lb-plus common came from an old estate lake where finding the hot spots proved very difficult.

for silt fishing when one would appear to be enough? After all, silt is just silt isn't it?

Is Silt Just Silt?

Silt isn't just silt and I hope you all understand where I'm coming from when I say that. It varies in depths around our waters as well as in age. It is formed in a number of different ways, but more often than not by deposits of leaf matter, which are then broken down naturally by organisms found in the aquatic environment. The older a lake is, the deeper the silt usually is, but the important thing to remember is that age does not affect the richness of the food found amongst it. In many cases a lot of the nutrients a water environment needs are locked up in the silt, hence the reason that fisheries' consultants lime silty areas to assist with nutrient control.

In a newly dug gravel pit (twenty years old or less), silt may be found only in very isolated spots. These spots may be only an inch deep. Finding isolated pockets like this could lead to the gold mine areas we all dream about. The leeward side of a gravel bar may be one such spot, or perhaps the windward end of the water has a bay surrounded by trees. What about areas

A peanut hookbait that had been resting over some thick black silt for less than twelve hours.

where reeds and weed are abundant? Have such areas developed naturally or has man intervened? Naturally occurring weed areas may be silty on the bottom, hence the reason that weed roots have established there. On the other hand, the weed may be rooted to baskets sunken by man. Are there any reedy bays? If so, what's the bottom like there?

Plumb the depths, check the bottom. Use close seasons to your benefit and research the lake when the fishing is closed, so long as the officiating club will allow. Make note of your findings and make sure that, come season time, you use your information to your advantage. A standard plumbing set up will help you so much I can't stress its use enough. Better still, check the depths with an echo-sounder and compare your results. A grey-line facility on an echo-sounder will help you to pin-point with amazing accuracy where any differences between hard and soft bottom may lie. They will also tell you the depth of silt you have, which is invaluable for telling you where you may get a better form of presentation, or indeed where you may find any

old black smelly silt – the stuff that stinks and discolours your hookbaits.

Some of the worst areas of rotten silt that I've come across were tight up against the dam wall at Jennetts reservoir in Devon. Here the depth went down to 30ft (9m) if I can remember rightly. In the deeper water the silt was almost like tar, but without the stickiness. It was dreadful stuff, jet black and stinking of decayed matter. It is a known fact in scientific circles that the deeper you go in water, the less life you will find to break down fallen leaf matter. These areas are termed anaerobic because the oxygen is being used to break down any matter that may be present, rather than any organisms. The breakdown of any matter will take longer than in shallower parts, and it is for this reason that fish usually avoid such areas. When I say this, I obviously mean without angling pressure. As we all know, angling pressure has a habit of changing even the most concrete of scientific facts. The carp may be driven down into the deeper areas by anglers' lines for instance. I know that this is what is happening at Cassien in France. In the north arm of the great lake, depths range down to over 100ft (30m). Some of the best carp captures are now being taken from such depths as the fish move into these areas to avoid pressure from lines.

Although the whereabouts of the carp and where they will feed in a water is determined by so many different variables, we can make the assumption, as I said earlier, that if silt is present in a water, it will be – or will at some stage have been – investigated by the carp. Some spots for sure will be more attractive than others, and my findings indicate that these are more often in the shallower parts than in the deep areas. Shallower spots offer so much more potential when it comes to the sort of food items that carp love. Mosquito larvae such as bloodworm prefer the shallower areas to lay their eggs, as do many other important aquatic organisms. In fact, most of the life in our waters is found in the shallower spots because light penetration (the sun's energy) dictates this. The more turbid a water, the shallower a lot of these organisms will be found, and the carp will certainly recognize this.

Where Do They Feed?

I have made the point that very silty waters may not only be the meres or estate lakes. I know of gravel pits that are so silty it makes you wonder whether or not they are gravel pits. I also know sand and clay pits of a similar nature, but the big difference with these

sort of venues compared to the meres and estate lakes is their other characteristics: they offer a different form of environment, one that is usually frequented by man in all sorts of ways because they are normally found close to road or railway networks. They are also used for a multitude of activities, such as boating, dog walking, cycling. and so on. Estate lakes and meres on the other hand, are generally found in isolated locations, locations that are usually very private and quiet – so quiet in fact, that I'm damn sure the biggest hurdle anglers face on these waters is the surprise factor. Carp can sense man's presence at all waters, but in estate lakes, where man is normally not present every day, the fish are far less

A group of big carp make their presence known at a Shropshire mere.

An estate-lake 33lb mirror makes its only mistake of the year.

accustomed to the sounds made by man, which of course makes things more difficult for the angler.

I know from talking to a lot of anglers that on very silty waters it is the firmer silt patches that many prefer to target. I can only think that the reasons for this are mainly to do with the presentation aspects. Although such areas do frequently produce the goods, I can't help but think they are not necessarily the best to target, unless, that is, the firm patch is found in a deeper depression – indicating frequent disturbance by fish. On silty waters, especially the meres and estate lakes, the food larders are sometimes locked up in the silt as much as a couple of feet down. This is where the larvae such as the bloodworm feel safest depositing their eggs. They are protected, so to say, from predators, helping to ensure successful reproduction – something that all animal instincts revolve around. Whilst bloodworms can be found all over the bottom of our waters in the warmer months, it is the larders that contain the most, and these are the spots I'm talking about. These are the spots that the fish home in on and dig up the lake bed for.

In my experience, the foraging of carp means the food larders tend to be found in areas deeper than the surrounding bottom. They may be only a couple of inches, possibly 2ft, deeper, but where they've been discovered there will almost certainly be a difference in depth. I remember finding such an area on Wergs Hall, a water in Wolverhampton. I found it more by chance than anything else. It was an old estate lake venue, very quiet and secluded. The spot lay in the middle of no-man's land really. It was just out in the middle of the lake. It wasn't small, though, covering an area of around 18sq. ft (5sq. m). I banked half a dozen fish off it the first time I found it. Four months later I'd had almost fifty, including one of the venue's biggies.

I also discovered a few during my time at Orchid Lake in Oxfordshire, albeit somewhat smaller and isolated when compared with the venue in Wolverhampton. Although a gravel pit, and totally different to the previous example, Orchid is fairly silty in places. One day, whilst drifting along the reed line in a boat, I happened to notice three dinner-plate-sized areas that were totally clear of weed and somewhat deeper than the surrounding bottom, which was very silty in between the weed beds. I marked the spots and duly caught from one of them within twenty-four hours. One of these I caught from each and every time I fished the water over the next six trips. They were the foraging holes of the carp, and were only three of many that I went on to discover around Orchid. I remember talking to Paul Bray about these spots when he used to be the fishery manager. He once told me that you always knew when the carp in Orchid were on the bloodworm as you would end up with a scum from the silt on the surface of the water. This scum was normally visible for two or three days after the fish had fed and was a great indicator of where the main shoal of carp would be. I have made the same sort of finding on several silty type waters since.

Annual Hot Spots

Another important observation I have found over the years, and one I know that many anglers have written and talked about, is the annual cycle of hot spots. Some areas of silt are productive on a short-term basis, only changing when anglers discover them; others can be altered by the annual cycle of the seasons. As summer turns into autumn, some silty areas change from productive to terrible. An area of silt that has produced remarkable results since the start of the season may all of a sudden stop being such, only to return the following season. Most lakes have them. Although they can change for any number of different reasons, it is usually the seasonal weather patterns that affect them the most.

Probably the biggest influence on these sort of areas, especially when it comes to silt, is the warmth of the sun. Sun, as we all know, has a massive effect on all things related to life. In water, it determines the abundance and location of food items for the whole of the aquatic environment. The fish may regularly visit certain areas of a water during the summer because of what they will find there. This may be food; it may be comfort. Conversely, they will leave areas alone because they are not desirable.

I have found that some silty areas, especially those found in shallow water and collection points for fallen leaves, lose their effectiveness when the new leaf matter starts to fall and autumn arrives. This is not to say that carp will not visit these areas when this happens – far from it – but I do think they don't root around in them as much as at other times. They will visit them, picking off any visible food items,

I caught this same 29lb 12oz mirror the following year from exactly the same spot I landed it on this occasion.

only to leave them once they realize the environment of the area has changed. Possibly the covering of the leaves makes the foraging of the bottom difficult. More probably, the alteration in the water quality where the leaves are breaking down not only makes the area, can we say, 'unpleasantly smelly' to the carp, but quite possibly uncomfortable to the food items that the carp feed upon. Although this can happen to any area of bottom, I do think it happens more obviously in silty spots which are collection points for leaves as this is where the breaking down and production of chemicals is more abundant.

It all sounds complicated stuff, but the point I'm trying to make is that an understanding of simple freshwater biology makes fishing over silt a lot clearer. All food items of fish go through an annual cycle of

Partiblend seed mix available from Hinders, a great base feed for fishing over silt.

A great alternative to the seed blends is Formula Majic pellet.

availability, and this, in turn, alters the productivity of certain areas of the lake.

The Silt Game

One of the best types of bait I've come across for silt has to be particles. I've had so many memorable sessions over silt using tiny seeds it is usually the first bait that comes to mind when I'm confronted with silt. Tiny seeds, such as hemp, dari – or the now readily available blends of seeds like Partiblend – would always be my first choice, but I will admit that the type of fishing I do a lot of these days doesn't always lend itself to their use: I find myself rushing around a lot, and I tend not to plan my fishing as much. Probably the biggest and best alternative I've used is Hutchy's Formula Majic pellet. I love this pellet. It has been very kind to me when particles would suit the situation but I've not had any with me (bad planning happens to all anglers). I won't turn this into an advert so I'll just skim the reasons why FM has been kind. It is a blend of crushed particles – need I say more!

My main reason for choosing tiny seeds, or pelletized seed, for fishing over silt is that they resemble the types of food that carp

feed upon in these areas. They are small enough to excite the grubbing instincts of carp. They tuck themselves away into little crevices, getting the carp rooting around. They also prolong the feeding spell as the fish need to work to achieve satisfaction. They lend themselves rather well to all types of silt situation, whether it is food larder indentations (which I prefer to concentrate-bait) or just 'no-mans-land' areas of silt (which I like to broad-bait).

Although we all have our preferred bait, I must admit that I have caught well on several types. Like so many things in carp fishing, bait choice should be governed by the situation you are confronted with. Silt varies from water to water and also from-swim to swim. A thin coating of silt may allow the use of a heavy bait, whilst a thicker waftier patch may swallow it up. For confidence reasons I like my baits to be visible to the carp as much as possible. With the tiny seeds, I use these in large quantities of at least 4½lb (2kg) in the swim at any one time. I can't see any other way to use these baits without losing their advantages.

I must admit that I'm not a big fan of boilies for wafty silt, although I have caught with them when the mix has been modified or when I've blended the baits up in a food mixer to create small particles. To make the bait lighter in weight, an ounce (25g) or so of shrimp meal is a good additive to a dry mix. If you have never used the stuff, always experiment with it first as it is one of those ingredients that really can ruin a bait. Too much and the baits will float. You need to balance it out depending on the other ingredients included. Test your mix at home, or alternatively get one of the rolling companies to do the job for you.

There are times when single hookbaits will out-fish my preferred baited areas, but this is where your thinking cap comes in and you have to fathom out how best to tackle the fish on that day. It is hard to generalize but, looking back at my results, single hookbaits have been better in the areas of anaerobic silt (the deeper areas of water) – the areas where the carp wouldn't normally feed upon natural food. A glugged pop-up of a couple of inches (5cm) has worked well in these situations.

When it comes to rigs, probably the biggest question you hear anyone ask is 'Bottom baits or pop-ups?' I'll come to this in a moment, because before I touch on that topic I may as well comment on the weight of the rig as this is very much the same as bait. You need to get things right for the situation. Leads sink into silt. Heavy leads sink even further than light ones, especially when cast. This may sound obvious, but silt fishing isn't just a case of attaching any old rig and lead and away you go. Some situations will require stealth, such as a float fished worm, while others will require a long-range set-up.

I have caught carp over silt on critically balanced baits, pop-ups of an inch (2.5cm) and 6in (15cm), bottom baits, small baits, particles, big baits, and so on. I like to keep things looking as natural as possible. I do prefer bottom baits where I can get away with them, but there aren't many types of silt that are hard enough to keep this type of presented bait very visible. I'm a big believer in the idea that carp rely heavily on their sight to feed, so for silt I do have a tendency to use pop-ups more than anything else. To give you something to go on, I probably use 2in (5cm) pop-ups the most. A lot of the silt I have come across has at least an inch or two of suspended surface layer – not all, but enough to make me realize I would be stupid offering bottom baits

Particles really can get them frenzying over large areas of silt.

Boilies blended in a food mixer make another great alternative to particles.

A 29lb 4oz common from the Mangrove Swamp in Shropshire – another victim of the
Uni-Rig, this time presented on a longer link of 15in to combat the silt.

more than pop-ups. Two inches makes a
bait sit proud above this suspended layer. If
it isn't present then I don't think I lose anything by offering a pop-up, as the hookbait
will be lost amongst the mass of tiny seeds
that the carp will see in the area.

The practicalities of offering seeds on
the hook are very difficult, but if you use

Kryston's Bogey this excellent product
allows you to offer a boilie type presentation. The smaller the ball of Bogey the better. I like to roll a ball of about ¼–½in
(8–12mm). This can be presented as a pop-
up by using a cork ball in the middle. I also
have no problem using this over the top of
Rod's Formula Magic. I just roll the cork

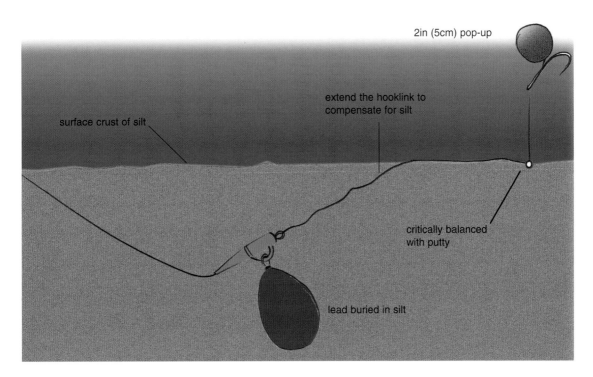

Rig for silt fishing.

ball in Bogey and then in the particles, compress it all down to ensure that it stays in place, and then balance or weight it.

For most of my silt fishing I use my trusty favourite Uni-Rig. All I'll do with this is take into consideration that the lead may sink into the silt, so if I'm using a preferred length of hooklink at that time (say 12in), I will add a couple of inches to allow for the sinking of the lead. This applies to both boating out hookbaits as well as casting. If I'm boating out, I'm usually fishing at extreme range, in which case I will be using a very heavy lead to keep the line tight. Heavier leads, even when dropped lightly from above will make their way into the silt after a while, especially when you start to tighten up from the bank.

8 Carp Food

There is no such thing as an advanced carp bait, so this chapter is basically going to focus on my thoughts on some of the widely discussed bait issues of the modern era. I think it's fairly safe to say that if you exclude French holiday venues, most of the adverts that appear in the angling magazines are connected with bait. There are loads of bait companies around today, and perhaps equally as many rolling firms, all offering anglers a great choice, but perhaps making the decision of which to use slightly difficult. Choosing the right bait is all about confidence, something that newcomers may be lacking. I am one of those anglers who never pre-decides what bait to use because you never can tell what mood the fish will be in on the day. There will be times when you will need to use boilies and there will be times when you will need to use particles or pellets, or even a combination of all of these.

I tend to use particles more in the summer and autumn months than at any other time of the year; I use boilies all year round. I will also use boilies in small amounts as well as large quantities, but I will usually use particles only in mass baiting situations, a time when I think particles come into their own and become a truly devastating bait. For me, boilies make up

Hutchy's ready-mades. Confidence in a bucket.

You'll need a lesson in science to understand the thinking that goes into designing the modern-day carp bait.

Confidence in a carp food is a must. A mid-thirty from the ultra-tough Withy Pool in Bedfordshire.

about 80 per cent of my bait, so most of what I shall talk about in this chapter will centre around these. I use boilies more than I do any other bait because I believe that they can give me an edge over other anglers more so than particles and pellets. Although they can be chopped up, flavoured, as well as bought in various sizes, particles will only ever taste of particles, and because of this I don't think they offer much in the way of individuality when compared with boilies. I can style a boiled bait to a chosen size, as well as flavour it with whatever ingredients I like to make it taste different.

At the moment I use only Venture products. Of course I've used several other manufacturers', especially the Rod Hutchinson range (which has been incorporated into almost all modern-day carp baits). Ask Rod a question on bait, and he can answer it straight away. It doesn't matter what the subject is: whether its flavours and their composition, or base mixes, he'll answer it off the top of his head. Most of my thinking on bait is therefore similar to his.

Basically my baits have to be attractive both visually and chemically and at the same time taste good to the fish. Carp fall for baits as much for their taste as for their attractiveness, and it's easy to overlook this fact. The attraction properties of a bait stimulate a carp's interest in it. If it then samples it and likes what it tastes it's going to try another, and then another, even if it isn't particularly hungry. I have several favourite chemical attractors including Monster Crab, Scopex, Esterblend 12 and Esterfruit. I'll back these up with additives such as Shellfish Sense Appeal, Amino Blend Swan Mussel or Liver Extract, all of them unique blends with qualities of their own. As for dry-mix ingredients, my favourites are liver powder, egg biscuit (found in several birdseeds), Robin Red, white fishmeal, calcium casienate, and yeasty type products like the old PYM (Philips Yeast Mixture). Each of these has its own benefits, with most being attractive to the taste buds as well as having some form of waterborne attraction (to send the food signal to the carp). I always like a birdseed and fishmeal combined in all of

There are now loads of commercially ready-made base mixes on the market, all with their own unique blends of ingredients.

my mixes, although I will vary the levels depending on weather conditions, water type and confidence at that moment in time. I also like calcium casienate in every bait, too. I rate this product a heck of a lot, not just because it's soluble but because I believe that carp just love the taste of it.

BEING DIFFERENT

Talk of specific ingredients and compounds reminds me of the level of thinking that goes into designing carp baits today. Bait is now a science, and a market that is changing all of the time as new breakthroughs are made. Each year there are new products coming through – products that have been tested in the field against some of the toughest carp in the land and for hours on end by some of the world's leading anglers. It therefore stands to reason that anglers wanting to advance their catches use something that gives them an edge – something that the carp have not seen for a while, or simply one that is slightly different and individual. Most anglers today use ready-made commercially available base mixes rather than designing their own, usually getting a rolling company to make the finished bait for them. Instead of following the crowd, I like to include a few additional ingredients with a mix before rolling, or tweak it by adding appetite stimulators or blending different flavours and additives together.

Another thing that a few of my mates and I have been playing around with a lot in recent years is blending two different base mixes together, something that isn't exactly new but that is still not carried out by many other anglers. Most anglers have at one time or another played around with different flavours and liquid additives, but very few, even today, play around as much with mixes, especially since it used to be a

You could say that this one has certainly been on the munch!

kind of rule that a mix was a sacred blend of ingredients.

I remember running low on a birdfood mix in the late 1980s. I couldn't get any more of it in any of my local shops so I rang a famous baitmaker, who I won't name, and asked his advice on mixing it with some 50/50 mix and some fishmeal that I had in the cupboard. The advice I was given was a firm 'No' since any alteration to it would upset its balance. I've always been into the bait side of the sport and I wasn't convinced by his words, even though he'd caught countless more carp than I had, so I took a gamble and thinned it out with some Richworth 50/50 mix and Hutchinson Seafood Blend. The result was I ended up with one of my best catches ever at the water I was fishing, including the capture of a common that had never seen the bank before. That one result alone gave me the confidence to play around with different mixes, tweaking them here and there with low levels of ingredients to try to give me an edge on the waters I was fishing.

The world of bait is still very much a 'secret' one, but trying things for yourself is a great way of breaking down barriers. I am convinced we can still find some great edges by experimenting with combinations of different mixes or by adding our own little touches. The Addicted & MC Mix combo, which a lot of people are now using, is just one example. We stumbled across that by sheer chance. Many of us, myself included, take the rolling companies for granted these days. I don't like the hassle of rolling my own bait any more so I have someone else to do it for me. I rely on The Bait & Feed Company to do everything, a firm that delivers the bait freshly rolled to my door within a matter of hours. I called the company to order some Addicted, but they hadn't enough left for my order. They had some MC Mix in and so we decided to mix the two together, even though we'd never done that before with these two mixes. I first used it at Raduta in October 2003 with Steve Briggs, and we had a terrific result.

Take the strain out of making bait by using one of the established rolling companies.

The great man Steve Briggs with one of his many Cassien lumps caught while testing the MC Addicted mix.

We then gave it to John Lilley, who caught some great fish, and then it passed a proper test at Cassien in the winter when Steve Briggs and his wife Joan had their best winter ever on the place.

In fact, Briggsy mentioned something very interesting to me quite recently while we were talking about that very trip. He had found that the action came throughout the day and night, something that he firmly believes was to do with the bait he was using. It was a sure fact that the fish had not seen the Addicted/MC Mix combo up until his trip, and as it turned out there were no defined feeding patterns like there usually are. The blending of the two mixes possibly helped promote this, firstly by tasting different (which is why there was no distinct feeding pattern – it stimulated hunger when the fish wouldn't normally have been feeding), and secondly, perhaps, by doubling up as an attractor (some of the ingredients were soluble), one that the fish also hadn't seen before.

I wouldn't say that any combination of mixes will work wonders in any session, or

Storing carp food in the freezer is by far the best way of keeping some of the active ingredients fresh.

Air-drying – another great way to keep bait fresh.

that by tweaking a bait with a little bit of this or that will either, but if you are willing to experiment a little, eventually I'm sure you'll find something that will prove its worth. I have messed around with all manner of different baits over the years, and I know several others who have also done so. No one gets it right every time, but one thing that keeps anglers like me searching is the knowledge that carp learn through association, and that the best way to overcome their shyness is to find something they want.

FRESH AND NUTRITIOUS

Making a fish pick up the bait in the first place, though, is a matter of more than just composition. A lot of modern carp baits have been termed active baits, basically because they contain enzymes that promote the digestion and taste of a bait. Products such as The X-Cite, Activ-8, Shellfish B5, Trigga, F1 come alive within the first seventy-two hours of preparing them, something that you just can't get

with a shelf-life bait. To get the best from any ingredient or additive in these baits, you need to use them as fresh as you possibly can. As a result, freezer baits are extremely popular – anglers believing they give them an edge because their attractiveness to carp appears to be enhanced when they are used fresh.

The freshness of a bait also affects its nutritional content, something that I think also has a bearing on a bait's attractiveness. Not everyone agrees that HNV (High Nutritional Value) baits have any particular appeal, but if the fish can associate something with danger then surely they can associate something else with benefits. The HNV theory has never tried to make anyone believe that carp can look at two baits and decide which has high nutritional value and which doesn't. It's more to do with the long-term benefits once the food source has been established.

179

Who says fishmeals don't work in winter?
Action at Orchid Lake with the MC Mix in
late January.

and cereal-based baits do, even when you
store them in plastic bags to keep the
moisture in and then defrost them slowly.

Storing fishmeals for longer than twelve
months is also said to be unhealthy for the
carp. Although fishmeals are a very successful additive, baits containing them have
received a lot of criticism over the last fifteen years: some anglers say they cause
long-term problems with the carp's im-
mune system and as a result aren't successful in cold weather. I won't argue that it is
easy for carp to digest fats in cold water
because it isn't. The gut flora that helps
with the passage of fatty foods through the
intestine becomes less active the colder the
water becomes. All the research I have seen
in journals about the reaction of the carp's
gut flora in cold weather, though, has been
carried out with carp from intensive fish
farms (being bred for the table). In the
papers I have read there were concerns that
carp being fed high-oil pellets (designed for
trout farming and containing anything up
to 70 per cent fishmeal) as their sole food
source were causing a poorer-quality fish.
But before such a comparison can be used
alongside angling we have to accept that
fishmeal baits can be classed as such simply
because of their fishy smell. So overwhelm-
ing are some fishmeals that a mere 5 per
cent in a mix will make it a fishmeal bait in
the minds of most anglers – hardly the
same as 70 per cent. To add to this, I don't
know of any carp waters that compare to
intensive fish farms. At IFFs the carp are
on the move all day long owing to the
nature of their environment (small space,
large biomass). They are artificially fed
every day and these environments are so
different to the lakes and waters we fish
that there really is no comparison.

There is no disputing that high levels of
fat in the diet of a carp can cause damage
to the liver, but there aren't any baits
around that contain the same levels of

Baits containing fishmeal and milk pro-
teins, especially, have a limited shelf-life.
They degenerate quite quickly and I never
re-freeze them once they've been rolled and
frozen once. I also won't keep them for
longer than twelve months in the freezer.
Some boilies freeze really well, but I always
find these baits turn mushy the longer you
keep them. They also have a tendency to
suffer freezer burn more than birdseeds

fishmeal as the traditional trout pellets used for farmed fish, so it is not an issue. A bait containing more than 40 per cent white fish, capelin, salmon, or whatever, will not bind or roll very well, especially through the machines used by the rolling companies, so baits have to be balanced out with other ingredients. We also have to accept that lake carp will feed on other food items, too, so their diet will be far more balanced than those of fish in farms. The whole debate about fishmeals in winter can be put to bed quite easily by considering the number of fish that get reported each winter in *Carp-Talk*. Why does the magazine continue to be inundated with catch reports by anglers using fishmeals if the rumours are true? Well there's only one answer to that question: fishmeal baits catch carp all year round. It is a fact that only the foolish would argue against.

It is always great to know that anglers care so much for their quarry that they go to the trouble of checking out what is and isn't good for them, but my opinion is that we do have to be sensible about earmarking something as not good if we can't back up our statement with facts. I can speak with confidence that all of the baits I use are of a high nutritional value. The X-Cite, The MC Mix, and others such as The Yellow Seed Mix and Liver Mix, are all well formulated with reliability in mind. All of them catch fish but, most importantly, they are designed with carp welfare in mind, something that perhaps best explains why all of Rod Hutchinson's baits have become legendary within the carp fishing industry.

MATCHING BAIT ADDITIVES
An interview with Rod Hutchinson

A look at the bait scene would never be complete without some sort of interview with the biggest name in carp baits, Rod

Give me a nutritious bait any day of the week!

Hutchinson, the man that brought us such legendary bait additives as the original Scopex, Monster Crab, Chocolate Malt, and the highly successful Sense Appeal range. In this interview, Rod finishes the bait chapter nicely by talking about the four seasons and how matching your bait to what's going on in nature is the key to designing the ultimate carp-catching foods.

Simon These days, you have various bait companies selling base mixes designed for certain times of the year. Do you think this same line of thought can be applied to flavours?

Rod Absolutely. You can also do it with other forms of additives, such as the Sense Appeal range, sweeteners, and appetite stimulators.

Rod, passing on his knowledge to the younger generation.

Simon   Give us a few examples?

Rod   I think in the spring months, when the carp are leading up to spawning, they need protein to build up their reserves and tissue. There's a time in the spring when they tend to munch on everything so I like to try to simulate the natural food sources at this time of the year. This is more diffi-cult to do with base mixes, so the additives are the best way. I never try to overload flavours in the spring. This is the time of the year when the aquatic system is full of all sorts of messages from natural food. The fish know there is food about. I prefer to use flavours at very low doses, instead emphasizing the Sense Appeals – the food stimulants rather than messages. Flavours I look at as being messages, which, like I say, are very abundant in the water during the spring period.

Simon   Do you have any favourites that you use in spring?

Rod   I don't experiment much with addi-tives these days. I did that in the past. I know what works best, and I have total faith in Regular Sense Appeal and Shellfish for the spring months. Some of the overseas lads also have great faith in these, and some of the hardest waters in the world have responded to this line of thinking in spring.

Simon   What about summer then? Does your thinking change from the spring?

Rod   Yes. This is the time of the year that I rate flavours very highly. I rate flavours as calorific to the carp. They are food. The carp are on the lookout for food more in the summer than they are in the spring. In the spring the food is there and multiplying.

Early-spring action from using one of the Sense Appeal additives in a bait.

In the summer it has already been grazed on. My favourite summer flavours tend to be those that are sugar-based, such as Propylene Glycol, which is a water solubolized sugar, or Glycerol. In fact most forms of sweetener are good summer additives. Thick hydrolysed sugar is brilliant. I've got a short list of summer flavours, such as Chocolate Malt (a sugar compound), Maple Cream (which is very underused but has turned over some of the hardest waters in England and abroad in the summer), and Super Cream. These three are superb, simply because they give the carp what they want at that time of the year.

Simon What about autumn and winter? Is your thinking specific for these months of the year as well?

Rod Again yes. The four seasons are so different that it's always going to be wise to change the angling approach as the year progresses. The natural food cycle is different month to month and, like I said earlier, this is what I use as a guideline. I'm always trying to mimic the food sources that are natural to the fish. In most venues this is the natural food stocks of bloodworm, crustaceans, mussels, crayfish, and so on. As autumn comes around, my way of thinking is that waters are generally lower in oxygen at this time of the year. Everything in the water is breaking down as the water cools down. The leaves on the trees enter the aquatic cycle at some venues. These require oxygen to break down. I generally think that as the oxygen levels fall, water-soluble flavours and additives are better. My Ethyl Alcohol range is what I turn to. Strawberry Dream and Cinnamon are excellent autumn catchers, as are Leaf Spice, Mandarine and Autumn Harvest. I tend to place more emphasis on flavours in autumn. I'll cut back on the Sense Appeals, usually by half. The carp are normally hungry in autumn as they recognize the depletion in available natural foods and the

Mally Roberts talking bait with Rod during the filming of the Hutchinson *Four Seasons* DVD.

need for fats and protein for the winter. I don't need the food stimulants, rather the message of 'Here's some food'. They'll be on the lookout during the early part of autumn, but there will be very little of it around.

Simon And for winter?

Rod My thinking on the base mix front changes in the winter, and with this so do the flavours. I'll normally use a high-protein mix in the winter with a citrus flavour. Sometimes I may opt for a loose-textured base mix, such as a birdfood base combined with an Ethyl Alcohol flavour, which really come into their own in the colder months. They are highly soluble, which is what is required when water temperatures are low. In the winter, Glycerol flavour bases are one of my least favourites. These tend to thicken in cooler water, much like oils, and are virtually useless in my experience.

Simon Continuing with the flavour theme, Rod, do you think that today's carp angler can become lost amongst the many flavours that are available? You've mentioned in this interview some of your favourites, but there are others on the market that go under the same flavour names but are totally different to yours.

Rod I think that many of today's anglers accept that our company is one of the originators and therefore one of the most reliable. There are some very good flavours available from other companies, and mine may be looked at as just one of the many on the shelf, but none has the history of development that our flavours have. I don't like bragging but that's a fact. I was the first to bring out flavours using Glycerine ester, Tryacetin and Diacetin. Others copied later and claimed that these were the key to carping success, but they aren't. All waters are different and, most importantly, the diet

requirements of the carp change throughout the twelve-month period, so no particular flavour bases are really the key. Some compounds of fruits and sugars come alive in these bases, such as the ones that can organically produce these esters naturally. Like I've already said, the key to the flavour issue is helping nature along its natural path.

Simon Aside from flavours then, can you finish off by telling us about Secret Agent?

Rod Believe it or not, I left this product on the shelf for three years before I did anything with it. At this moment in time, my thinking with Secret Agent is a bit different to what it was when I first released it. We've had some excellent results with it since its release, but I'm having some fabulous results with it at a level of 3ml rather than my originally recommended 5ml. I don't know why this is, but I'd hazard a guess that it has something to do with the food message that it's releasing to the fish. People have to remember that Secret Agent is a blend of organic and amino acids. It is therefore unique. It is a feeding stimulant for carp, rather than just a food message like flavours. It has nutritional benefits, which is where I believe its edge lies. So successful has it been that I firmly believe that even the smallest amount in a bait can be detected by the carp. I may even drop my levels this winter to as little as 2ml per kilo.

Secret Agent has been designed not only as a stimulant for carp but as a mimic of the natural foods found in the aquatic environment. This is why, I believe, it is proving to be so successful in smaller doses. Carp have very refined sensors and can locate tiny bloodworm beds, so, in reality, there isn't much need to overdose with the additives in the winter. The key to winter fishing is really to do with finding the fish rather than giving them a heavily glugged bait.

More than 10,000 acres (4,000ha) of water, but Secret Agent pulled this mid-forty to the hookbait at the famous Lac du Der Chantecoq in France.

The whole issue with additives is very simple, Simon. Anglers just need to look at nature and try to match this as much as possible to the foods that the fish feed upon in a particular water at certain times of the year. This is what I've been trying to get across for years. My bait range is based on this theory, and so is my fishing.

Simon Cheers for talking to us, Rod. I know there'll be a few anglers changing their approach once they've read this. Excellent.

9 Hookers

If you've made it this far into the book you will probably have gathered that I like to keep my carping as simple as I can. My approach to hookbaits, however, is a bit different as I tend to faff about with these more than I do with anything else in my carping arsenal, making sure they are exactly right and acting as I want them to when cast into the middle of a lake. To me, the hookbait is the most important piece of my kit, aside from the obvious things such as rods, reels, and so on. If something isn't quite right with this department, there's just no way a big wily fish is going to sample it.

THE SCENT THING

Before I even attempt to try to explain some of my thoughts on hookbaits, can I first touch on the topic of smell. Carp can smell, or sense, things quite differently to the way we do. They have very, very refined receptors all over their body, enabling them to 'smell' even the most minute trace of scent. I recently read a feature by Frank Warwick in *Carpworld* magazine stating that he advocates washing your hands in lake water or rubbing them through the lake-bed silt before you start messing around with bait on the bank so as to mask any scent that you may leave on the bait. Frank gets my vote 100 per cent there. To humans, carp have a unique scent about them, as do roach, bream, tench, and so on. Surely a creature with even better defined

receptors than we have could say the same about us?

I learnt a big lesson on this subject some fifteen or so years ago. It happened while I was watching a group of six mid-twenties feeding on about 3 kilos of bait during the opening week of the season in 1991. The fish had been fed the same bait for around twelve weeks, mopping the stuff up like there was no tomorrow. As I sat there in a tree, I was amazed to see the fish eat the lot bar two hookbaits that were amongst the bait and around ten to fifteen other close-by freebies. Without even sampling the hookbaits, they had singled them out to avoid. It took them about three hours to do this, and it was amazing to watch. I couldn't fathom

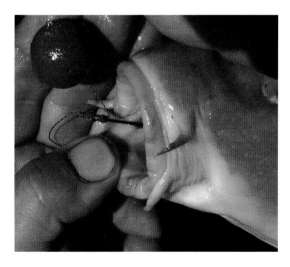

If the carp doesn't like the smell and appearance of a hookbait, you aren't going to catch it.

How defined are the carp's receptors? Can they pick up the angler's scent on hookbaits and freebaits?

out what was wrong. The rig had been working well for me, and the hookbaits were made from exactly the same mix as the freebies, which they were apparently happy to take. This was early season and the fish were gagging for it, so the whole experience blew me away. Around the time this happened I was using a Coleman petrol stove to cook my on-the-bank meals. It was also at a time when Tim Paisley had written a thought-provoking feature in *Carpworld* about carp being able to identify danger through the smell a human leaves on a bait. The answer came to me when I realized that my fingers had been tainted with petrol from my stove when I handled my hookbaits. This tiny little detail had been the difference between my catching and blanking. The fish had smelt my scent, more specifically the petrol on the hookbaits and the adjacent freebies that they left behind, and they didn't like

it. I had baited up the marginal spot by hand, and the freebies the fish avoided were probably the ones that had been closest to my skin.

Since that day I have always washed my hands in lake water or taken a handful of boilies, broken them up, rubbed them over my hands and then discarded them before touching the hookbaits or free offerings that I intend to use. Having fished with Frank Warwick quite a lot since, I know that he too rates this scent thing as highly as I do. After attaching a new hookbait, he always boils the bait and rig in fresh water before casting just to clear them of any germs and unwanted scents. Some people will say that's taking things too far, but I can promise you that on the really pressured and difficult waters, it is this kind of attention to detail that makes the difference. Frank catches awesome amounts of fish, and I can say that since I have been as careful, my own catch rates have improved. Whether it's bottom baits or pop-ups, I will always be very careful how I handle my hookbaits, or the rig for that matter.

ON THE BOTTOM

I'd say that bottom baits perhaps make up around 70 per cent of my fishing. I much prefer a natural presentation so tend to use them whenever I think I can get away with them. This is usually when the bottom is relatively hard or firm, or where I think I'm not going to end up masking the hook or losing the hookbait in soft matter like silt or silkweed.

I tend to place waters in five different categories when it comes to angling difficulty. At the bottom of the scale are the real easy ones, such as your St Lawrence rivers; stepping up from these are your Catch 22s, then your Orchid Lake, then your Withy Pools, and finally your Yateley Car Park

I got it right on this occasion: a lovely mirror from the heavily fished Cassien in the south of France where the carp are as tricky as anywhere in the UK.

Lakes. On the easiest of carp waters where it is a chuck a fish, I've never seen much difference between standard bottom baits (straight out of the bag) and those that have been made with an insert to overcome the weight of the hook. The carp in these types of water tend to be hungry and very willing to take the hookbait challenge. At these venues I just take a bait from the bag, needle it, and attach it to the hair.

I start to jazz things up a bit on the bottom bait front when I'm targeting venues the next level up. On the Catch 22s, where the fishing is very, very consistent, the carp will have seen it all, but will be willing to take a gamble in order to satisfy their appetite. By doing something a little bit out of the ordinary when others around you are following the norm, you can reap rewards. I remember when Rob Hughes

189

A drag with the lead reveals that it is perhaps not a good time for bottom baits in this swim.

and I fished the Norfolk day-ticket water in 1994, catching almost seventy fish in just over twenty-four hours. Rob was using his then-favourite bottom baits with two poly-pop inserts while I went for ready-mades straight out of the bag – the typical tactic of the time according to fishery manager Phil Grey. By the halfway point, Rob was well up on me until I decided to follow suit. The carp hadn't seen poly-pop inserted hookbaits as much as criticals or out of the bag ready-mades, and that little difference helped no end. All we were doing was using 18mm hookbaits with two small poly-pops inserted to help overcome the weight of the hook fished over the top of the same-sized freebies. It was obvious that the carp had a similar strength vacuum suction and could single out the regularly used criticals and out-of-the-bag hook-baits fairly easily. By counterbalancing the weight of the hook, we were able to con-

fuse them somewhat on that particular day. Most of our catches were the same weight, low to mid-doubles. I don't know how long this consistent action would have lasted, but it certainly did the trick during that short space of time, and it has done the same on many an occasion since.

Most of my bottom-bait caught carp since have been taken on inserted hook-baits, similar to those I used at Catch 22, made by drilling out the side of the bait and inserting a piece of cork. These catch-es have included fish from tough venues such as Motorway Pond, Brickyards, Withy Pool, Dolly Mill, Hardwick and Cassien, as well as from numerous easy and middle of the range venues. I think that with bot-tom baits there are very few anglers these days who go to the lengths of counter-bal-ancing the hook with a couple of poly-pops or a slither of cork or foam. Most either use baits straight from the bag or criticals of less than an inch. For me, there's more to bottom baits than just these two presentations, and I think the carp have been getting away with it on more occasions than many of us would like to think.

I think one of the main reasons why inserted bottom baits aren't used much today is that you can't buy them ready-made. The angler has to go to some lengths to make them for himself, unlike pop-ups or baits from the bag. All I do is take my chosen hook – for UK fishing, generally a Hutchy Precision in the size 6 – slide a piece of cork onto the shank, and then immerse it in a glass of water. I bob the hook up and down in the glass checking its buoyancy – because even a small piece of cork can make a very heavy hook float if it isn't sunk beneath the surface. The water surface acts in a rather strange way with light objects in that it helps to keep some items afloat when they actually shouldn't be. If you sink them below this barrier, you'll see a different reaction, so I

Cork inserts are my favoured way of tweaking my hookers.

keep doing this until I have found the equilibrium. You usually find that the same-sized piece of cork will keep the same pattern and size of hook balanced. What I look for is the cork to just keep the hook afloat, then I either insert the right amount into a drilled-out boilie or wrap it in boilie paste and then boil.

POP IT UP!

As I have already said, I don't tend to use pop-ups as much as I do bottom baits these days. Over the years I've flicked from one to another as my favourite, and had varied amounts of success with both. As I've grown older though, I have been more drawn to the bottom baits because of the pressure cycle. I'm a stickler for trying to keep my rig and hookbait as natural looking as possible. If the carp in my target water have a habit of cleaning anglers out, leaving only the hookbaits, then I try harder to make my traps look, smell and taste like the free offerings. Yes, I firmly accept that at times, the angling situation just

Hookbait balancing tools are essential for tough waters where the fish can easily single out hookbaits.

Not the most natural presentation in the world, especially if all the freebaits are on the bottom.

I usually make all my own pop-ups so that I can make them to my own specifications.

won't let you do this, but I think that most of the time you can get away with it.

Despite my preference for bottom baits, however, I will always carry pop-ups with me whatever the weather or venue. Like most anglers, about twenty years ago I went to great lengths trying to make my own pop-ups. I just could not get them right. When microwaving was the 'in thing' I kept burning them. Then we had baking, which resulted in the same problems, and then we had ready-made versions. which to some extent were usable. I've never been happy with the commercially available ones, so I settled on cork ball inserts for quite some time. Although they took quite a lot of time to make, cork ball inserts at least allowed me to use a pop-up that was almost the same as my free offerings.

I used these right up until ten years ago, when Dave Poxon revealed the secret to making microwaved pop-ups. Instead of placing them in the microwave after boiling them, I had to do it while they were in the paste form, something that was a bit of a trade secret and never written about in the press. Hey presto! It was like a new world. No longer did I have to sit there

through hours of painstaking hand-rolling, I could almost mass produce pop-ups to my own specifications very easily, and I still do it to this day. I can even regulate my hookbaits to my preferred buoyancy by adjusting the length of cooking time. The longer I cook them, obviously the more buoyant they become. Criticals for twenty-four hours, or pop-ups for seventy-two hours, I can do the lot at the press of a button, and I haven't looked back since.

I still use some varieties of ready-made pop-ups because there are some excellent brands on the market. Rod Hutchinson, Venture, Nutrabaits, Nash and Mainline sell some very good ones, as do several of the bait-rolling firms and top bait companies. You only have to look through a copy of *Carp-Talk* to see for yourself. You can now get criticals, super-buoyant pop-ups or whatever you want in this consumer world we live in.

Although I use pop-ups only now and again, I still carry a variety of different types, sizes and colours with me. I love the bright yellow for the winter theory of Frank Warwick's, and I've also used it with success in the summer, too. There are times when a single pop-up fished all on its own in a patrol route area can be very productive, especially during times of hard fishing. I remember a few years back when I first fished Cassien. There were plenty of anglers present and hardly anything getting caught. Most of the lads were baiting heavily each day, but I fired out single hookbaits and within an hour of arriving two rods rattled off. I continued to catch throughout my six nights as well, which at the time was a nice result.

Used at the right time, pop-ups can be devastating, but used at the wrong time you'll suffer. My pop-ups come out of the bag the most when fishing silty waters or venues where it is possible that the hookbait will get masked. Blanket weed is very problematic in the summer, as is fallen leaf matter in the autumn, and I suppose I use them most at these times.

I have also had some good results with them when the carp are in an inquisitive mood and there are no obstacles to overcome. It's difficult for me to describe when these times are, but I really do believe that pop-ups can annoy carp if placed in the right spot. They will pick one up just to see what it is, or because it is annoyingly placed on a patrol route or feeding area – provoking a, 'Get out of my way' or 'What's this?' response. These are the times when I love

to use the bright baits that Frank has so expertly written about and used – usually during times of hard fishing, when the baited areas aren't working well, or when the fish are just picking up the odd freebie here and there. Sometimes a bait popped up a couple of inches over a baited area is the first one to be sampled, especially when using particles.

Experience helps you to identify the obvious times to use pop-ups, but the not-so-obvious ones can be tricky, as can deciding the height at which to set a bait. I tend to use pop-ups no more than 4in (10cm) off the bottom, although I will experiment at times. I suppose I use them at 2in (5cm) most often because this is the height at which light silt cloud lingers above the lake bed and places the hookbait out of harm's way and in full view. The same can be said for other bottom debris. Leaves don't lie any more than an inch or so off the bottom. Most of the time I will have dragged a lead before casting out just to make sure the lake bed is fairly clear, giving me some sort of indication of how high I should be presenting. The only times I tend to use pop-ups higher than 2in (5cm) is when I'm targeting patrol routes. I've had

There's some very good commercially available hookbaits on the market.

Used at the right time pop-ups can be devastatingly effective.

a fair amount of success on the big waters using them popped up between 8 and 12in (20–30cm), the height at which many carp travel from place to place. The intention here is to stop one in its tracks.

I am a big believer in overshotting pop-ups: not overshotted to the point that the hookbait is almost permanently fixed to the bottom, but so that it is at a similar weight to the freebies. Not so many anglers use this method these days since most prefer to opt for criticals – pinching off the putty so that they sink ever so gently. I use criticals only as single hookbaits, when the carp have nothing to compare the hookbait with. Criticals have been flogged to death on a lot of circuit waters and I think this overuse perhaps puts the odds back in the favour of the fish if you use them too much and not in the right way. Criticals act so, so

The master of the single hookbait theory, Frank Warwick, with an Orchid Lake mid-twenty mirror.

differently to overshotted baits. I've seen carp approach baited areas wafting their fins, tails and creating vortexes as they try to disturb the free offerings to see if any act differently to the rest. I have even seen them swimming into baited areas and almost scraping their flanks along the bottom (as though cleaning themselves of parasites) just to make the freebies spread and bounce along the bottom. Some carp really are cute, especially if they have seen one particular method time and time again.

WASHED-OUT BAITS

One form of hookbait that has scored very well for me in the last few years is the washed-out bait. This involves soaking a hookbait in lake water and washing out all of the chemical attractors, aiming to make it appear to the fish as though it has been in the lake for quite some time and is safer than those that smell strongly of flavour. I hear quite a lot of reports about the success of this tactic, and when one of the anglers advocating it happened to be Rod Hutchinson I had to include it in my armoury when I started fishing on the tricky Motorway Pond.

I rang Rod to update him on how I'd got on during one of my trips overseas and asked how he was doing. During the telephone call, I asked him about the methods he'd used to catch a 39lb common from Woldview, which had appeared in the *Carp-Talk* news pages while I was away. He told me it had fallen to his Addicted mix with no flavours or additional additives. To cut a long story short, he had decided to opt for the approach because, when he was catching, the action always came on the second day that his baits had been in the water, indicating that perhaps the fish were wising up to flavours. My recent trips to Motorway had seen me with tench and bream and

nothing else. The carp were avoiding me, to the point that I was getting a bit frustrated: during one trip I had one roll right on top of my bait, but nothing came from it.

It's time for desperate measures when you see carp in your swim but don't catch them, even at tough venues like Motorway. Why weren't they picking up the bait? They were obviously attracted into the swim. I knew it was not my rig, and even if it was I wasn't prepared to mess about with it. It had to be the bait or the way in which I was offering it. After the conversation with Rod I decided to try washed-out baits and, hey presto, as if someone had just flicked a switch, I started catching. I went armed with bait that had been soaking for two days in a bucket of water taken from my garden pond. There was nothing fancy about the method, or any other additives added. I decided to use pond water because of something my mate Frank Warwick had mentioned to me when talking about preparing particles: he advised me to soak them in lake rather than tap water since the latter contains a lot of chemicals to make it fit for drinking.

Washed-out hookbaits boiled in lake water can be awesome on the right venue.

Carp angling legend Rod Hutchinson with a 39lb Woldview common, caught with the assistance of a washed-out hookbait.

The method certainly did the trick. On my next trip I baited with a hundred washed-out 24mm Addicteds underneath an overhanging willow tree. I could bait the spot by hand without causing too much of a disturbance on the surface. I was fishing less than a rod's length out, so I could both bait up and place the rig into position very discreetly. After a couple of hours I was woken by a violent rod knock that almost lifted the rod from the rest. I sat there for an hour watching the rods, expecting one to blast off, but nothing

happened. I thought that the fish had singled out the hookbaits so I reeled in and dropped them back into position without any disturbance. This time I placed the hookbait in a different position, some 2ft (60cm) away from where it had been singled out, aiming to confuse the carp a little. Ten minutes later I had another violent rod knock before everything went quiet for half an hour. Once again, I repositioned, at the same time introducing a further twenty baits close by. I also opted to double up on the hookbait. I had been using a single

24mm on the hair, but this time I placed two on, which I hoped would help to confuse them a little more.

Half an hour later, just as I was contemplating packing up, the silence was interrupted by a singing buzzer. The left-hand rod was being pulled from the rest like there was a JCB on the end. Such was the power of the take that it had forced the rod out of the rest and the reel up against the buzzer. The carp kept pulling, so much so that the goalpost rod rests I was using went over the side of the front board and into the lake. I just managed to grab the butt of the rod and keep hold before it could disappear into the depths of the margin. I was struggling to keep hold of the fish, and at first I thought I had hooked into the venue's big-

gie. Nothing in the Motorway to my knowledge could power off like this fish other than a forty-plus. During the ten minutes that I battled, it went in and out of the corner snags about half a dozen times. I'd coax it out, it would power off back. I'd coax it out, and back it would go. This was the hardest fighting fish I had ever caught from the venue. When I first caught a glimpse of it, I just laughed. It was all of low-twenties! It was a fish, though, and that was all that mattered after six blanks on the trot.

I was back at the venue the next week, again opting for the same swim with the same tactics. It was almost a mirror image of the previous day because, a couple of hours in, I had a violent rod knock. This time my repositioning and re-baiting efforts

Motorway Pond, where I first experimented with washed-out baits.

A mid-twenty mirror from the Motorway on a bait that had been washed-out for forty-eight hours.

went unnoticed by the carp and I blanked, but three days later I was back. I couldn't get into the same swim this time because there was a match angler fishing, so I went for one close by – an area that hadn't received much attention for a while. This time it took only an hour for me to be woken by a violent rod knock. I was fishing locked up again, right in the middle of a thick set of pads. I had baited with about a hundred freebies, scattering these all around the pads hoping that they would get

the carp searching. Half an hour later I decided to reposition the hookbait similar to the way I had done the previous week. I fired it about 2yd away from where it had been. I had also armed the rig with a three-bait stringer. An hour later, I was in! As with the carp from the previous week, my rod was almost pulled from the rest as what felt like a good carp battled to get to the back of the pads. Steady pressure managed to coax the fish out, and I soon had it battling in the open water. Once again it felt

Motorway madness in the shape of a 33lb 8oz mirror.

like a decent fish, but this time it wasn't going crazy like the previous one; instead it kept hard on the bottom. It wasn't the monster I had wanted, and only turned the scales around to 23lb, but it was obvious that I'd worked the fish out, and that the washed-out baits and re-casts were helping to confuse them.

Since that season, the washed-out baits have gone on to catch me numerous fish from several tough venues, so if you ever feel that you need something different for your target water, give them a go. It's amazing how pressured carp will respond

to something as minute as a level of flavour in a bait, but they most certainly do.

TIGER-NUT HOOKBAITS

Although I use particles of all different types as hookbaits at one time or another, the ones I use the most are tiger nuts. I find tigers an incredible carp bait, so much so that when I was recently asked to recommend the one bait I would use to put my life on the line I chose these ahead of even the boilie.

The tigers I have been using in recent years have been either those supplied by Dynamite Baits or those prepared by the Bait & Feed Company. Both have been excellent quality and I fully recommend both brands if you are one of those anglers who likes the convenience offered by ready-prepared particles. I used to prepare my own all of the time, but now I am happy to put my confidence in others who make and prepare bait for a living.

I have had some excellent results on tigers fished directly on the bottom, but I generally prefer them popped up a couple of inches. I think this makes them more visually apparent to the carp, with the pop-up often being the first to go, even when they are presented over a large quantity of free offerings. I don't think this tends to happen as much with boilies, especially the bright-coloured ones, which are 'in the face' of the carp. Tigers and other particles have a habit of turning the carp on, making them root around a lot more.

For all of my particle hookbaits I like to offer them on a fairly large hook, usually a size 2 or 4. I think this size suits the amount I like to mount on the hair. I load this with as many particles as I can, along with a small section of cork, mainly because I like these hookbaits to stand out and look the biggest and most inviting. In the case of tigers I will select the lightest nuts in the batch. You can guarantee that at least one or two nuts in each handful will float, and these are the ones I select. I usually take a testing bucket with me to do this, filling it with water and then tipping in the baits. The ones that usually float tend to be the blacker sort. They are usually very hollow and spongy, whereas the sinkers will be harder and much paler in colour. Although I always add some cork to the set-up just to be sure, by selecting the floating tigers I will at the very least have a much more natural-looking presen-

I like to use tigers as multiple hookbaits, with three or four of them on a hair along with a piece of cork.

tation. To make some of the sinking tigers float, you may need a right wedge of cork, which will make the set-up look and perform totally unnaturally. This slight attention to detail might not matter on some venues, but at least it gives me the confidence that my hookbait looks OK.

I weight the pop-up down with some tungsten putty, usually offering it critically balanced. Most tigers are fairly light and the carp will suck several up in one visit to the baited area, so I don't want it to be too overweighted or it may be rejected because the carp are unsure of it. The only time I will overweight it is in shallow water (3ft/90cm or below) when there is a good chop blowing.

It isn't just over baited areas that I present tigers. I recently read a fabulous article by Ken Townley in *Crafty Carper* about using stand-alone hookbaits: he recommends the use of tigers as single hookbaits. I too have had tremendous success with tigers when used as singles, even in the winter time. A lot of people say that tigers are attractive to carp because of their texture and the fact that they are crunchy. I agree with what these anglers say, but I don't think that is giving tigers the total

Tip a handful of tigers in a bucket and pick out the lightest ones of the bunch: these make ideal pop-ups.

Tigers offer chemical and visual attraction to the carp – as well as crunch.

credit they deserve. I honestly believe tigers are very, very attractive to carp in other ways. For one, when immersed in water they definitely give out a sweet aroma that will last for hours in the swim and will stimulate the fish in much the same way that other baits do. I am sure this is why they can be exceptional when used as single hookbaits as well as just over bait. I won't go as far as to say that tigers are as deadly in the winter as they are in the warmer months when used alone, but I certainly wouldn't have any hesitation in using them in cold water if the other anglers around me were sticking to the now in-vogue fluorotype winter hookbait approach. There is a lot of mileage in being different, even in the winter time.

LIVE BAITS

The use of maggots as hookbaits is obviously nothing new to anyone, but it's fair to say that for a number of years they were really overlooked by carp anglers. Only in the last five or six years have they taken on some kind of fashion status, mainly through the writing and promotion of Frank Warwick. Frank is widely known for being very thoughtful about his fishing, and several good catches – especially on day-ticket waters on the Richworth Linear complex – helped him to establish maggots as a great alternative to the boilie.

I would say that using maggots for carp really finds its own niche when the water temperatures are at their lowest. Obviously maggots can catch carp at any time of the year, as can boilies and countless other baits, but when a carp is overwintering and almost static in its favourite winter hole, most baits have only their visual and chemical attraction about them. Maggots, on the other hand, move about, which in itself is a form of attraction. They are a live, natural-looking bait, and one that also creates a form of sound attraction on the bottom, which the carp will home in on.

Despite plenty of publicity by the likes of Frank, though, I'd have to say that even today only a small percentage of carp anglers use maggots, which is remarkable given how successful they have been. I was

Close-up on Maggot Presentation

1. Attach a hair rig to your hook, to which you should thread a small piece of yellow rig foam. The foam, which should be about the size of your small fingernail, is there to offset the maggots slightly. Next attach a small rig ring via a Grinner knot to keep the foam in place. Make sure it is quite tight to the shank. Take some 6lb hair braid and thread it through the ring. About 12in (30cm) will be enough. Allowing about 6in (15cm) each side, fix the hair braid into position with a firm knot.

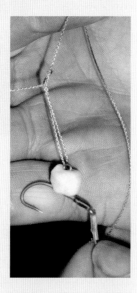

3. Take each end of the hair braid and fix the maggots into position shoelace style. Use a series of double overhand knots to do this. To tidy, trim off the two ends of the braid.

2. At one end of the hair braid thread a needle and begin to sew on some maggots. About twenty-five maggots will be enough. Slide all of these down the braid so that they sit right next to the rig ring.

4. The finished business end. Test that the foam counters the maggots to suit your presentation style.

Maggots are a great bait in the winter, offering the attraction of sound, which can often break the carp free of winter hibernation.

but – like everything in the carp world – in time, a method begins to establish itself. Opposite is a step-by-step look at how Frank Warwick uses this very successful bait. It's a bit fiddly, but it's well worth the effort when you see the results you can get.

ARTIFICIAL BAITS

Like maggots, artificial baits have only quite recently become a favourite of the carper. No doubt, you will have seen the Enterprise Tackle artificial sweetcorn in the shops because this bait has become so widely available since Terry Glebioska tempted Two-Tone on it from Conningrook at a British-record weight of 59lb 7oz in April 2001. There are other varieties, too, including pellets, mixers, maggots and particles. You can buy all sorts of different colours and sizes, from day-glow yellows, pinks and oranges – which are all made by a relatively new company called Alien Baits – through to luminous types made by Enterprise.

I personally favour the bright-yellow sweetcorn as well as the luminous type for static baits, both of which have a proven track record of catching in even the coldest conditions. Like the high-vis boiled baits, the luminous and bright colours all lend themselves best to being used as singles or alongside small PVA bag traps. A single grain, or two side by side, balanced out with a small shot would be my approach, especially on the waters that are quite well stocked. Don't let their plastic smell and texture put you off either, because it certainly doesn't seem to deter the carp. However, if the smell of them does affect your confidence in any way, a booster or dip of some sort would be useful here.

Believe it or not, the artificial baits I use most are the plastic pellets and tiger nuts. I don't use these for static bait fishing,

once fishing next to Frank at St Johns when he landed a rake of fish in February. He had kept the spod working regularly throughout the day, which I think was a big factor in his success. I doubt very much whether a single maggot hookbait fished alone would ever be as tempting to a big wily old carp as a nice carpet of wrigglies on the bottom. Getting the most out of this type of presentation requires a bit of effort from the angler, sending out half a dozen spods at intervals in the vicinity of the hookbait, which is perhaps why a lot of anglers still opt for boilies.

There are of course loads of different ways of presenting maggots on the rig,

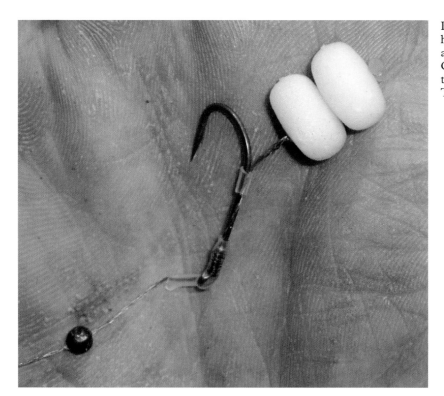

Plastic corn first hit the headlines when it accounted for Terry Glebioska's capture of the British-record Two-Tone at 59lb 7oz.

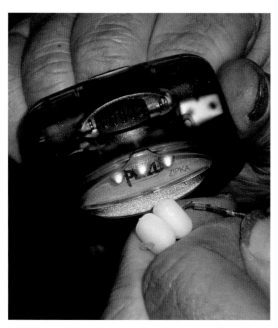

Luminous corn: light them up and away you go …

preferring both for surface fishing. Enterprise make an artificial mixer that to be honest hasn't produced me many carp off the surface. I have used it at tough waters on several occasions and the carp have just laughed at it. I don't know why this is so, but when I've changed over to the pellet or tiger nut both have produced me fish. From below the water they must appear to sit on the surface better, almost at the same buoyancy as the freebaits because they have both been instant catchers for me. All I do to mount them on the hook is take a brand new hook from the packet and force it through the plastic bait, eye-end first, almost directly through the middle. I do this so as to hide the shank of the hook, leaving just the bend and the point visible. (Pushing the point-end through instead makes the positioning of the hookbait a bit off-track and it then sits strangely on the surface.) All that's left to

When the carp has nothing to compare the hookbait with, boosters can steal you fish that otherwise may not be interested in feeding.

Baits soaked for long periods are ideal for use over stinky black silt, or when you plan on leaving your hookbaits in position for long periods.

do then is tie the hook to the rig, which I do by using a simple tucked blood knot.

GIVE IT A BOOST!

Especially when single hookbait fishing, boosters and dips are a great way of increasing the chemical attraction of the business end. These days you can buy ready-made dips for all seasons from most of the carp bait manufacturers, but generally these are made up of flavours or nutritional supplements such as amino compounds, so if you want to save a bit of money why not try making some for yourself?

One point worth noting about boosters is that not all attractors are as effective in the winter as some people will lead you to believe, so it pays to pick and choose which

you go for when the temperatures are plummeting. Instead of just going for the type that smells nice to you, go for flavours made from an Ethyl Alcohol base. EA flavours are much more soluble in cold water than, say, the widely used Glycerol type (the most common flavour base used), and will therefore be much more effective pullers of dormant carp. The Glycerol flavours tend to thicken the cooler it is, a bit as oils do, so they don't distribute very well in the water column. I leave some hookbaits in a dip for several days to soak up the smell, then store them in the rucksack for when the time is right. I like to use these when fishing over stinky silt or when I'm planning on leaving my hookbaits in place for upwards of six hours. Any shorter than this time and I'll just dip a fresh bait for five minutes or so as I set the rods up. Too much flavour can act as a repellent, I'm sure, so I prefer using boosters and dips when single-hookbait fishing so the carp have nothing to compare them with.

10 Holiday Carp Fishing

The types of lake and strains of carp in the UK are not quite the same as those found in some warmer climates. The fish in the UK therefore don't grow to the sizes they do in countries like France and Romania. Since the early 1980s – when news first reached us about Lac de St Cassien containing carp above 70lb – UK carp anglers have been travelling all around the world in search of new horizons and experiences.

The early pioneers to overseas countries helped to spread the growth of carp fishing all around the world, and much of the early continental carping was done on large, challenging reservoirs similar to Cassien where the weather had as much of an impact on the fishing as the carp did themselves.

Since those early trips, hundreds of companies have set about offering anglers far less demanding new experiences in foreign countries – a kind of holiday away from their local lakes. As a result of this increase in choice, the number of UK anglers now travelling overseas has increased dramatically, and there are now masses of British carp angling tourists.

The wilderness that is continental carping – an incredible ocean of adventure.

Some of the more experienced ones opt to travel alone and visit the less commercialized waters while others make the most of the booming commercial holiday market.

In this chapter I'm going to introduce those of you who fancy trying an overseas carping holiday to the types of trips that are available, the companies who specialize in offering them, and the gear that you will need if you go.

ALL-INCLUSIVE TRIPS

These are the trips that take the strain for you and introduce you to a country. All you have to do is drive yourself, along with your gear, to a pick-up point in the UK and board a coach or minibus, which then drives you to a lake. Food is included in the price (usually delivered to your swim) and these trips are regarded as holidays as much as anything. The fishing tends to be on private, commercially run waters of a size similar to the waters you find in England, and the fishing can be very intense but excellent fun.

The carp stock tends to be very high at the type of water offering these trips, with the average size being around 25lb. There are extras also available such as bait, tackle hire or whatever, but the more you want the higher the price will be. So popular are some of the destinations that many are fully booked for a number of years in advance.

On the downside, if you want to experience the solitude that overseas carp fishing can bring then these trips are probably not for you. All-inclusive trips by their nature can attract the 'instant' carpers who have very little experience and are mainly on the trip as part of a jolly with the lads. Sometimes the lakes can be very busy waters, not leaving you much time to yourself. Bear this in mind. These trips can be a great introduction to holiday carping, but you just might be better off driving yourself to a less-pressured venue.

All-inclusive usually means that everything is provided for you, including delivery to your swim!

Further your horizons with a trip to a big French water.

TOURS

These are probably the longest established of the holiday trips, dating back as far as the mid-1980s when the great Lac de St Cassien was discovered. Back then, Paul Regent offered coach trips to the south of France, and anglers were then left to do their own thing upon arrival.

On these trips, guiding is usually offered as an extra service – unlike the all-inclusive packages where it is essential. Most people who go on tours tend to be slightly more experienced and seeking a form of adventure the next level up from all-inclusive. The fishing tends to be on the more typi-cal French venues, many of which are somewhat larger than British waters – rarely less than 20 acres (8ha) in size and usually over 100 acres (40ha). Food is not usually provided, and anglers tend to pay for the transport. There used to be several companies offering this service to waters such as the heavily fished Lac du Der Chantecoq, but now most have broadened their horizons and offer trips to rivers and less-pressured reservoirs.

You may find yourself at a huge water containing some massive fish, or you may find yourself at a venue that is rarely fished. Whatever the venue, you will be placing a lot of faith in the organizer, so make sure you go with someone well recommended. Don't expect to catch dozens of fish on these trips, but expect the trickier and very credible fish instead. The tours give you the best insight into wild continental carping and usually the angler who enjoys one of these eventually starts pioneering for himself.

DRIVE AND SURVIVE

The majority of French venues in the commercial market fall under this heading, but obviously you can drive to any venue on the continent. You may have to book in advance to get a place at a premier venue such as Rainbow Lake but, generally speaking, the cost for this type of trip is a lot less than the all-inclusive or tour type. You arrange your own ferry or train travel for your trip, although there are many companies around today that will do this for you. It all depends on how much effort you want to apply to save yourself a few quid.

Some of the best-known drive-and-survive commercial venues include Lac la Horre, Fishabil, Rootswood Fisheries and Abbey Lakes. These are just a small selection, but any water can come under this heading if you don't mind doing a bit of looking. This is how I have made most of my contacts in France and also how I am able to fish venues that very few other anglers visit. Take a map, and if you find any blue water on it, ask a few questions in the local area

A superb brace of forties from big French reservoir Lac du Der Chantecoq (also known as Chanty).

and go for it. You will blank a few times, catch a few times, but you will also experience some of your best overseas fishing.

By a long way, driving is the best way of fishing overseas. Never go unprepared though. Set a destination in your mind, and work from there.

COME FLY WITH ME!

There are quite a few destinations that can be accessed by flying. Canada and the USA are certainly the biggest market and there are upwards of a thousand British carpers heading off to North America each year. Obviously flying is very different to travelling by car because you will be limited to what you can carry. You will be hit with a weight allowance of around 20kg for European destinations, 30kg for America, but if you book through angling tour operators this may be slightly higher to allow for the extra gear. For instance, the trips to Lake Raduta in Romania run by Angling International have an allowance of 50kg per person but, believe me, this isn't enough for one week of fishing on that kind of lake.

Most of the Canadian and USA operators offer you hire of fishing gear at the other side so you don't have to take it with you. This saves a heck of a lot of weight. I have been on three trips where the gear has been included in the price. These were to Canada with Paul Hunt's Canadian Carpin, to Lac de St Cassien with The Cassien Experience, and to South Africa with African Gold. On all occasions the gear was in exceptional condition. It had been looked after extremely well and was checked each week by the company to see if it was up to standard. The gear was top of the range European style carp fishing gear such as Hutchy or Fox rods, Shimano reels, Fox line, Nash hooks, and so on. Bait was also available on these trips, which is a bonus, and for the Canadian trip full board was thrown in since we didn't need to fish any of the nights.

If gear is not provided, a good tip is to get a Bazooka rod tube. This excellent piece of kit will safely protect your rods, landing net and banksticks during the flight. You can get them from most retail outlets, but if you are struggling then contact the Tackle Box (*see* Useful Addresses). Alternatively, you could try some of the excellent three-piece rods that fold down small. I've never used these rods but I have seen them and they really are the business for flying. They come supplied in their own little rod tube, which can be fastened together or sent through airport check-in individually.

For the trips to Lake Raduta I thin out everything I take so as to save on weight. The tackle box weighs a ton and is not necessary, so I put all of my bits and pieces into a plastic bag. I take the scales out of their pouch, and I rid myself of the packaging for anything. To give such things protection I wrap them in items such as my sleeping bag. So much weight is accounted for by items that are not needed that you can save almost half by being ruthless. I have even made myself a flight rucksack, which has no back carry straps and only a shoulder strap. I cut the back carry straps off because they weighed over 3kg – amazing!

I have heard of so many problems when flying that I always carry my most important items (other than my rods) as hand luggage: buzzers, reels, echo-sounders and my camera always stay by my side to prevent loss. Since the terrible events of September 11th 2001 there may be problems with doing this when flying to America, but it is always worth trying.

GEAR AND TACTICS

Whenever I do a slide show or talk about fishing overseas, people ask questions about

There are thousands of UK carp anglers now travelling to Canada and the USA each year. The St Lawrence river boasts some of the best carp fishing in the world.

the type of gear you need. Bear in mind that most French carp fisheries, certainly the ones run by British holiday companies and aimed at newcomers, have been set up as British carp fisheries in France but with French-sized carp, if you get my drift. They are therefore no different to the majority of waters at home. There are exceptions to this rule, obviously, such as Rainbow Lake, which is quite a daunting venue with its numerous features, but most are just shallow waters with plenty of carp. The type of gear you need on these waters should not, therefore, be any different to the type you would use in England: 12–13ft carp rods loaded with reels of a size that allows you to cast a reasonable distance are adequate. I think we are in an era of carp fishing when most anglers possess large pit reels and rods with a test curve above 2lb, so don't fret about special rods and reels for these waters because you really don't need to.

The only time you will need to upgrade your gear is when targeting the really big reservoirs or when you decide that the time has arrived for you to do a bit of pioneering on the rivers and larger lakes. Even for these venues, though, most modern-day carping rods and big pit reels will suffice. The only items that require attention are the lines, leaders, end tackle, rod set up and baiting equipment (boat, echo-sounder, and so on). Numerous books have been written specifically on this type of fishing so I won't go into depth about it here (one of the best books on the subject being Tim Paisley's highly acclaimed *Carp!*). There is also *The International Carper* magazine, which comes out each month and will keep you up to date with developments.

Bait Type

Treat your overseas fishing, especially at the commercial waters, as you would a heavily pressured water in England. People talking about being able to use rubbish cheap baits for overseas fishing is really just a reflection of some anglers' naïvety. Overseas carp are no easier than English carp. Trust me on

A 48lb 12oz common from Lake Raduta, Romania. To reach this venue, flying to
Bucharest is essential.

this and forget what is said by anglers who
haven't been overseas – regardless of how
many English forties they have caught.

Commercial French waters especially are
very, very popular. Many are fished 24/7

every single day of the year. The majority are
fished 24/7 during the months of April and
October, but even in these cases the fishing
time is enough to make the carp fairly tricky
when they want to be.

Former British record holder Lee Jackson slips the net under a St Lawrence river common for Martin Locke. Standard UK tackle was all that was needed.

Essential Overseas Checklist

- A valid passport.
- Foreign currency relevant to the country you are travelling to or the countries you are travelling through.
- First-aid kit, including various-sized plasters, bandages, antiseptic cream, mosquito-repellent and antihistamine, butterfly strips, painkillers, and a snake-bite syringe.
- Mobile phone with overseas access. Contact your network provider for details of how to disable the overseas barring.
- Travel insurance.
- For European destinations, make sure you have completed the E111 form, which is available at post offices.
- Language phrasebook/dictionary.
- Angling permits. To be within the law, purchase all your permits before fishing.

Good bait will overcome most problems at these waters, especially when combined with a good rig, and when I say good bait I mean your Club Mix, Trigga, X-Cite, F1, Multi-Plex, Activ-8, and so on, and not your budget-type mixes. Let's not forget that most holiday waters are well stocked. The carp will be depending on anglers' bait for a good feed – the fish in Rainbow Lake haven't reached world-record sizes through natural food alone! They will be feeding on bait even at the times when the anglers aren't getting any action. At some waters you may be wise to get on the bait that the fish see regularly, such as Dream Lake Specials for the Dream Lakes complex or Richworth Multi-Plex for Rainbow Lake, so do your homework first because on more than one occasion I have made the mistake of believing that the bait I am hav-

ing success with in the UK will work anywhere overseas.

Back up your boilies with a selection of particles. Baits such as tiger nuts, maize, hemp and seed blends have such a good track record at most overseas carp waters that I would certainly advise having some as a base feed for mass- or area-baiting, and as an alternative to the boilies just in case they prove to be a bit slow.

Before I finish this chapter by looking at ten of the best holiday carp waters available,

Steve Briggs with a French 50lb-plus mirror. Quality bait and a good variety of it will sort them out at most commercial waters.

I'll just say that if you are a carp angler with a carp angler's mentality then fishing over-seas will be a great thrill, even if you don't catch as many big carp as you would per-haps like to. Don't jump in at the deep end to begin with. Do your research and work your way up the ladder package by package, venue by venue.

I have been travelling backwards and forwards for almost twenty years now, blanking on occasions as well as catching a few along the way. It as an addictive form of carp fishing and I keep going back because the world is a huge place with so many waters to try out and so many differ-ent angling situations to experience.

TEN OF THE BEST HOLIDAY CARP WATERS

Contact details for the companies listed here are included in Further Reading and Information, page 238.

The St Lawrence River, Canada

Perhaps the most prolific carp fishing in the world is on offer in Canada through Paul Hunt's Canadian Carpin outlet. Fully-inclusive packages are on offer, including airport transfers, gear hire and food, and lots of 20lb and 30lb carp. A quality company offering one of the best holidays available.

The Graviers, France

Run by well-known British angler Luke Moffatt, this Dijon-based complex was the home of the previous world record of 83lb (caught May 2005). There are two lakes on site, with the main lake being the one with the biggies (at least two seventies and three sixties). The fishing is tricky on the main lake, with tickets available only by prior arrangement. It is very similar to UK gravel-pit fishing.

Etang de la Croix Blanche, France

This is one of the up and coming venues, and sure to challenge the world record in time. There are two lakes on this complex, one of 6.5 acres (2.5ha) and another of 8.5 acres (3.5ha), both containing 60lb-plus fish. The complex record was landed

in the spring of 2006 at over 72lb. Trips are all-inclusive only and available through Angling Lines.

Abbey Lakes, France

At less than 2½-hours' drive from Calais, Abbey Lakes is one of the most popular short-break French fisheries. The fishing is run by well-known carp angler Rob Hughes through Angling International. There are two waters for carp on site – Fox and Heron Lake – both containing fish over 55lb and both extremely well stocked with 30lb-plus fish. There is a clubhouse and bar on site as well as showers and a tackle shop. Ideal for the angler wanting plenty of action.

Rainbow Lake, France

Home of the world-record carp of 83lb 8oz (as of January 2006) as well as at least five other 70lb-plus fish. Located at Hostens near Bordeaux, France, this venue is open

The Lake of Islands, Rainbow Lake, home of the world-record carp.

Derek Fell with a Rainbow Lake common, only ounces under 50lb.

for self-drive trips as well as all-inclusive packages through Rainbow Carp Tours. Also known as The Lake of Islands, this 100-acre (40ha) venue is suited only to the experienced carper. You must book in advance to fish, and you must book early to avoid disappointment.

Dream Lakes, France

The most famous French holiday complex bar none, Dream Lakes has been running since the early 1990s. Located in the Champagne region, there are five lakes on offer, with all-inclusive as well as self-drive

trips available. Showers, toilet facilities, a tackle shop and bar are all available, and there are countless big carp to well over 60lb to be caught.

Lac Serriere, France

Situated close to Limoges, this two-lake site offers both self-drive trips and airport packages (via Limoges airport). It is owned by long-time British carp angler Bob Davis, and offers carp to over 50lb in both waters. The main lake is 20 acres (8ha); the smaller, well-stocked one is 3 acres (1.2ha). It is widely regarded as a beautiful venue and is a favourite of top anglers Tim Paisley and Steve Briggs.

Cross Channel Carping, France

This well-established company is owned by Si and John Haldane, two well-known continental carp anglers. They offer fishing on Les Teillatts, home to commons well over 60lb. Twelve anglers are allowed on the 35-acre (14ha) venue each week, with fishing available through all-inclusive packages.

Lac Fishabil, France

This famous Brittany complex was the venue for two of the first three World Carp Cups. It contains a big head of carp ranging up to low-fifties, with the average weight around the mid-20lb mark. It has excellent facilities including an on-site hotel and bar, and tennis court. It offers both organized and self-drive trips.

South Africa

For the real travelling angler, South Africa offers superb carp fishing during the UK winter months through African Gold Adventure Carping Holidays. Run by ex-pats Merv Pennell and Martin Davidson, fishing is offered on several waters including the wild and beautiful Klaserie Dam, which is close to the Kruger National Game Reserve. This is the ultimate in carping holidays with superb side attractions such as white-water rafting, air ballooning and much more.

The wilderness of South Africa, home to leopards, lions and crocs – just a few examples of what to expect on the bank if you visit.

11 Day-Ticket Carping

Together with Rob Hughes I spent a number of years in the early 1990s travelling all over England reviewing day-ticket waters for *Carpworld* magazine. Most of our trips were for single nights or forty-eight-hour weekend sessions and, to be honest with you, I probably learnt more from fishing those venues than I have done at any other time in my career. You could never take a tactic that worked well on one water to another because every situation was different, as was every venue. Understanding that simple message has stood me in good stead ever since.

Overnighters and short-session fishing are perhaps representative of most carp anglers in the UK, so most of you will be able to relate to it – a few nights midweek,

Graham Slaughter with a lovely scaly mirror from Catch 22 in Norfolk.

in between work, or a quick trip at the weekend. In this chapter I'm going to take a look at ten waters up and down the country that offer open-access day-ticket fishing. All are well fished and high-profile within the sport, and each has its own characteristics that will offer you something a little bit different. They are listed in alphabetical order.

DAY-TICKET VENUES

Bluebell Lakes

Bluebell Lakes is home to Benson the big common, a fish that shook the British carp record weighing in at over 60lb! There are several waters on this Northamptonshire complex, with Kingfisher and Swan Lakes the two most suited to the serious carper. Kingfisher contains at least three 40lb-plus carp, including Benson; Swan has them to over 50lb (the best being a mirror known as The Creature). Both venues are heavily fished and offer moderate to difficult fishing.

Catch 22

Rob Hughes and I visited this Norfolk venue in the early 1990s for only one night, and both of us came away with more than thirty fish each under our belts. It is a heavily stocked water and ideal for the beginner carp angler who wishes to test rigs and baits. Tickets are available on the bank, but if you plan your trip in advance you can book an island swim, which allows you to target a no-fishing bank – one of the best areas on the lake. The biggest fish to date is a common of 38lb.

Cuttle Mill

Located close to the famous Belfry golf course in the Midlands, this popular two-water complex offers carp up to 40lb in its 5-acre (2ha) specimen lake. There is no night fishing allowed, with swims in the warmer months available only by booking. In the winter it generally quietens off, but you are still advised to book. Although very heavily stocked with twenties and several thirties, Cuttle Mill (aka The Mill) is a bit cramped, with pegs out in the water marking each angler's boundary line for casting. It is, however, very easy, and perfect for learning to overcome riggy fish.

Farlows Lake

Situated in Iver, Buckinghamshire, this popular gravel pit is perhaps one of the busiest day-ticket waters in the Colne Valley. It is full of features, including bars, islands, pads, weed, silt, snags, and so, and also boasts some of the best facilities available. Farlows has its own bar, tackle shop and café on the banks. It contains several big fish up to high thirties, with the average size around 20lb.

Hardwick Lake

Also known as Smiths Hardwick, this lovely water is run by Linear Fisheries on their excellent complex at Stanton Harcourt, Oxfordshire. Hardwick is quite a deep venue for a gravel pit, and it offers several specimen-sized 30lb fish to over 40lb. It is a thinking angler's water, containing some stunning scaly mirrors as well as hazelnut-coloured commons.

Old Bury Hill

This Surrey estate lake is perhaps one of the best-looking day-ticket waters in the UK (one bank is a SSSI – Site of Special Scientific Interest). It is quite a heavily stocked water, with lots of silt, pads and features. There is no night fishing allowed

The popular Hardwick Lake on the Linear Fisheries complex, home to some of the best-looking carp in the UK.

on the day ticket, with the best carp averaging around 35lb. It has an on-site café and tackle shop.

Orchid Lakes

Located at Dorchester on Thames in Oxfordshire, this 18-acre (7ha) gravel pit ranks as one of my all-time favourite day-ticket waters. Known as the Home of the Thirties, Orchid has everything you could dream of for a carp lake, with features galore. It has a stock of around 150 carp: twenties and around thirty 30-pounders up to 40lb. I'd rank the difficulty level of the fishing at this venue as moderate, and

absolutely ideal for those wanting to make the move from some of the easier waters to one that requires the angler to think a bit to fathom out the carp. It also has a café, showers and toilet facilities on site.

Oxlease Lake

This very popular, extremely easy water of around 50 acres (20ha) is on the Linear Fisheries complex at Stanton Harcourt in Oxfordshire. Said to contain some 2,000-odd fish, averaging in the high singles, with a dozen thirties up to 37lb, it is a mature gravel pit with lots of options, and it is perfect for learning the basics of winter fishing.

Yours truly with an Orchid Lake 32lb mirror caught in May 2005.

Selby Three Lakes

Perhaps the most famous of the northern day-ticket waters, Selby Three Lakes is on the outskirts of Selby, halfway between Leeds and Hull. It has at least a dozen different thirties and once produced a 40-pounder, a fish known as Lucy, although the biggest at the time of going to print is in the high thirties. It is quite heavily stocked, and the fishing is ranked moderate.

Willow Park

Like Oxlease Lake and Catch 22, Willow Park is another very easy water ideal for the beginner carp angler wanting a bend in his rod. Located at Ash in Hampshire, it is a mature gravel pit with hundreds of fish up to the low thirties, the average size being around 17lb. They feed very well in the cold weather, which makes this venue perfect for the winter carper.

12 Opening Week at Redmire Pool

Redmire Pool. A tiny 3-acre (1.2ha) water that is steeped in British carp fishing history, the venue where modern-day carp fishing was born. It is a water I have dreamed of fishing since I first read about the catches of carp angling legends Dick Walker, Fred J. Taylor, Eddie Price and the Carp Catchers Club.

In early June 2004 I saw a notice in *Carp-Talk* inviting bids for the opening week of fishing on the legendary lake. This traditional event takes place in England each year: the angler who bids the highest gets to fish the extremely private lake. For several years I had talked with friends about placing a bid to fish there, but had

The dam wall shot, a must for any visitors to the historical lake.

never done so. I was going through the difficulties of divorce at the time, and needed a bit of time on my own, so after seeing the notice in the magazine the next thing I remember was being on the phone to Les Bamford enquiring about the current state of play. What was the highest bid and what did he think it would end up going for? No one had actually bid when I rang, so I opened the account at the asking price. Three days later Les called back to say that only one other bidder had been involved and if I went a little higher I would get it. I upped my bid there and then, and later that day Les called back to say that my bid had been accepted and I could make my way down to the lake in two days' time. To say that I was like a kid at Christmas is an understatement! I'd been really fed up with my situation at home and this was just what I needed to pick me up. I was going to fish the lake by myself, unwind, and enjoy five days of nostalgia.

The following is a day-by-day record of those five days' fishing, an experience worth every penny I spent. I didn't catch any whackers, but what a place …

DAY 1 – THE ARRIVAL

Although I have read countless articles about Redmire in the past and know a little bit about the history off the top of my head, I didn't have much time to jog my memory before I set off on my journey. Looking back I really wish I had, because when I arrived I wanted to be taken back into the years of Dick Walker and Chris Yates *et al.* I wanted to know the names of the different swims and where all of the famous catches of the past had taken place. Walking onto the banks of the famous lake brought all of it back to me. I was blown away by it. It is indeed a special carp water that is exactly as I had imagined

it to be. Set right in the middle of nowhere, enclosed in trees, full of weed, gin-clear water – it was Redmire!

I arrived for 2.30 p.m. and had a quick walk around, trying to weigh things up. As I walked, at first I wasn't sure if I'd got the right venue. The directions were very clear, I knew I was at Bernithan Court Farm, but the lake looked so small I wasn't exactly sure that I wasn't on Little Redmire, a pond slightly downstream of the main lake. It looked tiny. Also, after my first walk around, I hadn't seen any fish at all so I did have a few uncertainties.

I had to be at the right place. The dam wall looked so much like the one I had seen in the books. Eventually, my mind was set at ease when I discovered the Redmire hut. Yes, it was the one I had seen pictures of. I opened the door and took a look inside. It

The famous Redmire Pool estate.

was like going back in time. The air smelt damp and everything looked exactly as I recalled it from photos. On the wall was the bailiff's telephone number and the famous logbook. That's all I needed.

I had another walk around, taking time to try to recall the names of the different swims, or should I call them pitches as they were once referred to in the days of Walker? The only swim I could recall for certain was the famous Willow swim where Walker caught his still huge and very famous 44lb British-record common. A small willow tree stood to the left, planted, I believe, in memory of the fiftieth anniversary of his achievement.

This time around I decided to climb some trees to see if I could make out any shapes below the surface. The water was flat calm and the weather very humid and sticky. The first tree I climbed was to the left of the Willow swim. In front of here lay the densest weed beds. If ever there was going to be carp anywhere, it was here. As I got to the top of the tree, maybe 30ft up, I was in a different world. All over the water out in front of me, for perhaps half the width of the lake, there were purple shapes resting in the weed. Some of the fish appeared to be very small, in the single-figure bracket, but amongst them there were certainly a few twenties and possible thirties. One particular fish, which was resting off the end of the fallen tree just to my right, looked to be approaching mid-thirties or perhaps slightly bigger.

After perhaps twenty minutes of watching the fish from the top of the tree I had another walk round, climbing as many of the other trees as I could to see what lay resting out in front of the different swims. After a full circuit, it was very obvious that

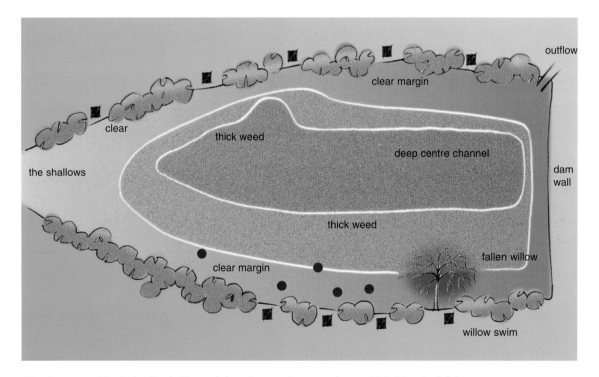

The features of Redmire Pool. The red dots denote the spots from which I hooked fish.

the majority of the carp were in front of where I'd first climbed, so it was in this area I decided to rest for my first night.

It looked to be a fairly tricky swim to handle. There were only a couple of very small clear areas amongst the dense weed. I didn't want to start chucking a lead around to see how deep it was or indeed to find out what the bottom was like, so it was going to be PVA bag tactics into holes in the weed for the first night to see what was what. I had some waders with me and, with a bit of care, I could reach the spots I fancied without creating too much disturbance. There was a small clear band of about 10ft (3m) wide between the bank and where the weed started, and that looked to be an option, too.

I could only get three rods in front of me owing to space, so I decided on a spot to the left in a small 3sq. ft (1sq. m) gap of weed about 10yd out, another to my right just on the edge of where the weed started, and the third out about 20yd (18m) to a larger clearing. I chose to start very light to begin with: Kryston Melt-Ex bags loaded with Formula Majic pellets and some Hi Betaine pellets from the Bait Company. Hookbaits were red MC/Addicted pop-ups of an inch, chosen to blend in with the reddish coloured bottom. It looked to be very shallow so I wanted everything to blend in because there was a very angry swan working the margins protecting a nest – the last thing I wanted to do was hook that thing and put the whole lake on standby!

I certainly got a better view as soon as I climbed a few trees.

Stepping back in time: the Redmire boathouse.

My rigs were fairly simple. Size 4 Hutchy Precision hooks, knotless knotted and then line-aligned to 25lb Kryston Super Nova. Because of the weed I went for in-line leads by Armaled, very light ones to begin with just in case I spooked the fish on the cast. I went for the 2oz size, but within half an hour had changed to 5oz because they weren't making their way down to the bottom. As I was lobbing out, the filled bags were acting as a buoyancy aid and were coming to rest about halfway down in the weed. I could tell what was happening, because as soon as the bags were dissolving a mass of bubbles was coming up from the bottom and the line was tightening up and pulling off a few more feet from the reel, which meant the lead was not on the bottom until after the bag dissolved. I needed to get it through the weed before it dissolved, ensuring my rig s were resting where I wanted them.

With all three rods in position, I sat back and set up base camp, as far back from the water's edge as I could. My experience of fishing small estate lakes like Redmire is that you have to blend in with nature and let the carp believe that there is no one present. It was very hard to do because the swims were tight and close to the water's edge, but I tried my hardest, switching off the mobile phone and even taking my shoes off to make sure I was as light footed as I could be.

I was all set and comfortable in the swim for about 9 p.m. The next minute, I was dreaming of Redmire monsters …

DAY 2 – GETTING ACQUAINTED

I didn't wake until 8 a.m. when I had a screaming one-tonner on my left-hand rod. I was not quite with it when I received the take, almost mesmerized by having had a 'take' from Redmire! When I eventually woke from the trance, I set the hook, at which point I could feel that it wasn't a particularly big fish. A tap, tap on the end of the line was all I needed. The fish weeded me at first, but after I donned the waders and coaxed it out it started to oblige. Just as I was about to get out of the water, however, it slipped the hook. I was a bit annoyed because I could have been on the fish faster and had a better chance. Perhaps my bait-runners were slightly too light, so I tightened them up a notch. What really bothered me though was that it was a missed chance. Last

The shallows and their chocolate-coloured water.

year at Redmire during the opening week, there had been only four fish caught. Last year in total there had been only 50-odd, so every one lost meant something to me.

I was amazed it had taken so long to receive a take. I really thought I would have seen one on the bank during the night, but it wasn't to be. I sat and watched the water for quite some time before re-baiting and slipping the rod back out. The fish seemed to be steaming past me by 8 a.m., as if they were making their way into the swim from the other end of the lake. Perhaps they had all been up in the shallows during the night. It was something I had to keep an eye on.

For most of the morning and the early part of the afternoon I wandered around the lake trying to stalk. It was far too warm for the carp to be interested though. It was well over 25 degrees in the direct sun, and the fish just seemed to enjoy lapping up the sunshine. Once again, as on the day before, I noticed a mid-thirty common resting on the edge of the fallen tree, all on its own, as if to say, 'This is my patch!'

By 7 p.m., I had re-baited all the spots with the same tactic. However, within half an hour I was on the move with all the rods because I had noticed the fish making their way out of the swim and heading towards the opposite end of the lake. I followed, and by 7.30 p.m. I had three rods on the bottom further up the bank, very close in, about a rod's length out, which is where most of them seemed to be patrolling. The other rod I was trying on the surface because I'd seen them taking the leftover Mixers that I had fired out earlier in the afternoon.

It was around 8.00 p.m. when I had a screaming run on a bag fished out of the swim known as the Style. I had decided to try a bright-yellow Fruit Frenzy pop-up on this rod, leaving the other two on the MC/Addicted. It was popped up perhaps 2in (5cm) and was attached to an angry Redmire fish. It took around five minutes to get it close to netting, by which time I could make out that it was a low-double linear mirror. It was a stunner, and very much resembled a fish I'd seen Jack Hilton

A dead simple rig was all I used on the bottom. An Armaled in-line lead combined with 25lb Super Nova hooklink and a line-aligned size 4 Hutchy Precision hook.

My first twenty of the trip – a classic Redmire common off the top.

holding many years earlier at a much bigger weight. On this occasion, the size was irrelevant: it was my first Redmire fish and I was well chuffed!

I re-bagged and placed the rod back in the same spot; about half an hour later, it was singing loud and proud once again. Another short tussle developed and then I was sat in front of the camera with another linear mirror, this time one of 16lb. At the time I knew nothing about there having been a recent stocking of fish into Redmire, but Chris Ball later informed me that Les Bamford had taken some of the spawn from the lake a few years previously and bred some small mirrors and linears in his stock ponds. These fish were introduced into the lake a couple of years ago as singles and were obviously what I had caught off the bottom.

Like my first fish from the lake, the 16-pounder had fallen for a bright-yellow

Fruit Frenzy hookbait, so without further ado I changed all of my static bait rods over to this tactic. I had taken the bright yellows with me mainly because I recalled Kev Clifford's amazing catches at the venue using sweetcorn in the 1970s. I concluded that as a result of that, almost everyone and his dog would have used sweetcorn since, especially a lot of the anglers who were at the water for only a week, so I opted for a similar looking bait, albeit chemically different. It seemed to be working.

After returning the fish, I wandered into the swim nextdoor to try some stalking on the surface. The fish in there were really going for the Mixers, although the light was fading quickly. There were five or six of them hoovering them down, so I attached a modified piece of an Enterprise Tackle plastic brown pellet to the hook and lobbed it out. I've tried the plastic Mixers on several waters in the past, but found that I have a better response on the top with the pellet. All I do with these is drill a hole through from one end to the other, and then, prior to attaching the hooklink to the hook, I slip it onto the line with a baiting needle. Once the hook is tied on, I then push the pellet down over the hook, making sure that the eye is buried inside. I like this presentation because I can make it so the hook is almost completely hidden, yet still has enough of a gap between it and the bait to catch well inside the mouth.

It took all of about five minutes before I was attached to my first Redmire carp off the surface. No sooner had it slipped up on the bait but it had ploughed through the biggest weed bed and almost to the other side of the lake! It 'took' that strong it completely flat-rodded me, stripping me of perhaps 40yd of line. It took a while to coax it towards me, but within ten minutes I had it under a bush at my feet. I slipped my trousers off and went in for it, and was soon making my way back to the bank with what

looked like a twenty-plus off the top. It was a classic shaped Redmire common, and was exactly what I had wanted to catch. On the scales it went 21lb 12oz, and when I told Chris Ball the following day he informed me that I had joined a rather exclusive club of only half a dozen anglers or so who had caught a Redmire twenty-plus off the top! It doesn't really mean anything in angling terms, but it did make me feel even more privileged to be on the banks of such a historical lake.

DAY 3 – ANOTHER TWENTY!

By morning my tally of carp had risen to five, including two twenties. I'd pulled out of two. All of them fell to PVA bags apart from the one off the top. Interestingly, all of the fish I caught off the bottom had come to bright-yellow pop-ups, and all less than a rod's length from the bank. Also, all of my recent fish had come from rods that were placed in swims nextdoor to where I was actually set up with my base camp. It was obvious they knew I was there, despite my efforts to keep myself as quiet as I could.

The two I had caught during the night had come at 1 a.m. and 6.30 a.m., my second twenty being the first light fish. It was a scraper twenty and I decided to carry it around to the dam wall where I could take some lovely photos of it in the early morning sun. It was quite scarred and looked to have been through a few battles.

As I returned it to the water, I noticed a group of five or six 20lb-plus commons congregating by the dam wall, close to where I'd slipped it back. Within an hour or two, all hell had broken loose out in front of where I was fishing. The carp decided it was time for a spawn as they thrashed the tops of the weed beds to a foam and really weren't afraid to show their presence. I just sat and watched, filming with my video camera and taking stills whilst sat in a tree. I got some brilliant footage and shots.

DAY 4 – TIGER STYLE

When I woke at 6 a.m., I knew I had a chance before 10 a.m. of another as the fish made their way back down the lake. The daily routine of the carp was becoming very obvious. By about 10 a.m. they were in the position where they would spend the rest of the day, until around 7 p.m. when they would start to head back.

After an early morning stroll I decided on a move to the Style pitch further along the bank. Although the fish did not seem to be interested in the shallows, there were a few lingering in the weed beds close to that area so it looked to be a better bet than my previous spot. My experience on old estate lakes such as Redmire is that it takes only a few hours of pressure in one area before the carp twig it and look for somewhere else to hang out. They really did like the weed off the fallen tree but they certainly weren't coming in as close as they had been at the beginning of the

A scraper twenty being photographed on the dam wall on my third morning.

trip. They seemed to be coming closer in further up.

Just after I had moved all the gear I was paid a visit by the bailiff, Richard Fox. Richard spent about an hour or so with me, which was nice because he certainly put me right on the history side of things. He reminded me of the names of the swims and the catches that had taken place from them. He fitted the bill of Redmire bailiff down to a 'T'. He was exactly as I'd imagined him to be, a well-spoken angler who fished with a cane rod and also did a little bit of fly fishing!

One interesting thing that Richard told me was that the fish liked tigers (tiger nuts) and that a lot of the better fish from the lake had fallen to these. I had a healthy supply with me, courtesy of the Bait Company, so as soon as he had departed I made sure I had a baited area out in front. Then I spent a few hours watching the fish enter and depart a large weed bed to the right of the Climbing Tree. I could get a really good aerial view of the area and I decided to drop a pile of bait right in front of one of the patrol routes. I baited with about 4kg of food, dividing the lot between

The view looking towards the dam end from the top of the Climbing Tree on Bramble Island.

two areas, again going in with the bright-yellow pop-ups over the top. I sat back for the evening, watching a bi-plane (which I'd seen on my first evening), doing some aerobatics in the sky. I really was drifting back in time, especially with the rolling hills of the Cotswolds in the distance and not a sound from anything other than a bird on the opposite bank, which I didn't know the name of and had never heard before at any other carp water!

DAY 5 – TAKE 5!

Twelve hours later, I was waking from my best night on Redmire: I'd had five takes, including my best of the trip at 24lb 12oz. Three had come from marginal spots, and the other two from the area I had located in the weed and baited with the tigers and boilie. The fish weighed in as two small singles and a 19lb mirror. I pulled out of the other take. The last fish, my biggest, had come at 9.30 a.m., weeding me in the process and demanding a bit of patience as well as the use of the chest waders. The Redmire carp needed a bit of persuading away from the weed, that was all. If you were careful, they would come through with ease. It was a nice finish to my best Redmire evening, and certainly my most atmospheric. I don't know what it was, but there was something special about my fourth night. The mist on the lake, the feeling in the air; there was something in my mind and it felt good.

For my final night I invited my old buddy Rob Hughes down for a look. Like me, he had never been to Redmire before. Although I had the lake for another three nights, other commitments meant that neither Rob nor I could spend any more time there. In typical Rob fashion, he arrived about three hours later than he originally said he would but, when he did, he was

The Climbing Tree. You could get a really good look over the shallows and the whole lake from the top of here.

The Style swim, moments after battle with my biggest Redmire Pool carp.

taken aback by the place as expected. He was like a kid at Christmas, too.

Shortly before he arrived I'd tracked some fish up the top end. They were really showing in force in the shallows. In the previous days they had barely ventured past the end of the weed beds in front of the Climbing Tree, but now they were right in the clear area of the shallows. They were also showing close in off the opposite bank. My side had gone dead, apart from the odd fish still showing by the fallen tree, probably owing to the pressure I had placed them under. Nothing was coming in close any more and I really did expect a blank for my last night.

When Rob arrived we crept up into the Field swim and watched some fish that were patrolling very close in. I'd had them taking Mixers close into the bank, but I didn't pursue them because the biggest was perhaps around 17lb and I wanted Rob to have a good chance of catching one, especially since he was down for only one night. It was amazing watching Rob set up: he even switched his mobile phone off as he crept around, so desperate to catch one! Anyone who knows him will know that switching his phone off is a rarity! After helping Rob to set up, I went off to sleep around 10.30 p.m.

DAY 6 – FAREWELL TO THE LEGEND

My final night proved to be uneventful, as I expected. Rob on the other hand was successful. He took his first Redmire fish at just short of 5lb. He was very excited about it, even showing me some digital pictures he'd taken. This was what Redmire was all about – he must have landed the smallest

Just as the bailiff had predicted. At 24lb 12oz, my biggest fish of the week fell to tigers.

One for the future, my biggest mirror. What
a stunner!

fish in the lake, but it was a Redmire fish,
and that was what mattered.

In total, after five nights of fishing, I'd
ended up with eleven fish on the bank and
three lost. Five of the fish were singles,
which had perhaps spawned from last
year, three were doubles to 19lb, and three
were twenties.

With that, we started to pack up, taking
some shots of us both on the dam wall for
the photo album before we s aid our
farewells to a wonderful piece of carp fishing history. Redmire is so very special.
Only Redmire can be Redmire.

The final morning and Rob fills in the
Redmire Pool diary, kept in the hut.
Farewell to a remarkable venue.

Further Reading and Information

BIBLIOGRAPHY

Ball, Chris, *The King Carp Waters*, The Crowood Press (1993)

Hughes, Rob, and Crow, Simon, *Discover Carp Fishing*, The Crowood Press (2002)

Strategic Carp Fishing, The Crowood Press (1997)

Hutchinson, Rod, *The Carp Strikes Back*, Wonderdog Publications (1983)

Paisley, Tim, *Carp!* Angling Books Ltd (2002)

USEFUL CONTACTS

Supplies

Eric's Angling Centre, Leeds
Tel. 01132 602033

The Tackle Box
Tel: 01322 292400
www.tacklebox.co.uk

Holiday Operators and Information

The St Lawrence River, Canada
Canadian Carpin
Tel. 001 613 534 2448
www.canadiancarpin.com

The Graviers, France
Luke Moffatt
Tel. 0 03 338 023 3539
www.lukemoffat.com

Etang de la Croix Blanche, France
South Africa
Angling Lines
Tel. 08712 004466
www.anglinglines.com

Abbey Lakes, France
Angling International
Tel. 01948 880884
www.anglinginternational.com

Rainbow Lake, France
Rainbow Carp Tours
Tel. 02380 392895 or 0775 2886319

Dream Lakes, France
Tel. 01206 76757
www.DreamLakes.com

Lac Serriere, France
Contact Bob or Sheila Davies, tel. 003 355 508 2645

Les Teillatts, France
Cross Channel Carping
Tel. 0208 3091009
www.crosschannelcarping.co.uk

Lac Fishabil, France
Starmer Baits
Tel. 07799 348614 or 01268 690300
www.starmerbaits.com

Day-Ticket Venues

Bluebell Lakes
 Tel. 01832 226042
 www.bluebell-lakes.co.uk

Catch 22
 Tel. 01603 872948

Cuttle Mill
 Tel. 01827 872253
 www.cuttle-mill.com

Farlows Lake
 Tel. 01753 655909
 www.boyer.co.uk

Hardwick Lake
 Tel. 07885327708
 www.linear-fisheries.co.uk

Old Bury Hill
 Tel. 01306 877540
 www.bury-hill-fisheries.co.uk

Orchid Lakes
 Tel. 01865 341810
 www.orchid-lakes.com

Oxlease Lake
 Tel. 07885327708
 www.linear-fisheries.co.uk

Selby Three Lakes
 Tel. 07818 092420
 www.selby3lakes.com

Willow Park
 Tel. 01726 860220

Index